First published in 2012 by Prion Books

This edition published in 2017 by Carlton Books
20 Mortimer Street, London W1T 3JW

7 9 10 8 6

A catalogue record for this book is available
from the British Library.

ISBN: 978 1 78079 974 8

Printed in Great Britain by CPI Group (UK) Ltd, Croydon CR0 4YY

THE OLD ONES ARE THE BEST

OVER 500 OF THE FUNNIEST JOKES ONE-LINERS AND PUNS

MIKE HASKINS

CARLTON
BOOKS

Introduction

The old ones are the best, as a famous footballer once advised a new customer at his local house of ill repute.

And there are certain areas of life where the old ones definitely *are* the best. These include fine wines, mature cheeses and great paintings. There are however other areas in which the old ones may not be quite so appealing. These include bottles of milk, erotic dancers and leaders of Germany.

But is it true of jokes that the old ones are the best? Well, why not have a thumb through the following pages and decide for yourself? Here you'll find hundreds of jokes, not a single one of which should come as a surprise to you!

Yes, if you've been paying any attention whatsoever during the course of your life, you should have heard all these jokes before!

But does that mean that these gags have lost their ability to amuse? Not a bit of it!

If you like and cherish a good joke, you will find the jocularities contained herein to be like dear old friends.

You may not have seen or heard from them for many years but now you can welcome them back into your life, have a good old laugh with them once again and introduce them to your loved ones (whether they want you to or not)!

And not only will you meet some old friends, you will journey back to a forgotten world as these geriatric jokes summon up a marvellous, old fashioned landscape.

It's a world populated by vicars, old ladies, cheeky little boys, simple farmers, courting couples, military personnel, polite shop assistants, pub landlords, foul mouthed parrots and well-endowed yet extremely friendly young ladies.

Admittedly there do seem to be an unusually large number of mothers-in-law, burglars and even cannibals living in the vicinity. There is also the distressing sight of dogs with no noses running about the place (and take it from me, they smell terrible!) And for some reason, men in this land invariably congregate in groups of three (even though they are often of three completely different nationalities).

But don't worry. If there's anything you don't like, you can easily get it changed. Just use one of the many genies in magic lamps dispensing wishes that you will find lying around the place.

So come on! Let's jump aboard the steam locomotive of laughter and travel back to the land of real jokes!

Just don't forget to bring as many light bulbs as you can carry – they seem to need replacing with remarkable frequency!

Mike Haskins, 2012

The Very Oldest Jokes In The World

The University of Wolverhampton was commissioned by the TV Channel Dave (the home of witty banter and endless repeats of Top Gear*) to compile a list of the world's oldest jokes. Among the jokes they identified were:*

The king goes to the court barber who asks him how he would like his hair cut. "In silence!" replies the king. *(from the Philogelos or* The Laughter Lover, *a joke book compiled in the 4th/5th Century AD)*

The Emperor Augustus is out on a walkabout when he notices a man in the crowd who bears a striking resemblance to himself. Intrigued, the Emperor asks the man, "Did your mother ever work in service at the Palace?" "No, your Highness," says the man, "but my father did." *(credited to the Emperor Augustus 63 BC – 29 AD)*

When the Cyclops asks Odysseus his name, he tells him, "Nobody." So when Odysseus's men attack the Cyclops, no-one comes to help him because he keeps shouting: "Help! Help! Nobody is attacking me!" *(from* The Odyssey *by Homer 800 BC)*

Q: What animal walks on four feet in the morning, two at noon and three at evening?

A: *A man. He crawls on all fours as a baby, walks on two feet as a man and uses a stick in old age*

(from Oedipus Rex *by Sophocles, first performed in 429 BC)*

Another source of ancient jokes are the Middle East stories about Mulla Nasrudin. Nasrudin is believed to have lived in the 14th century and according to some accounts was jester to the Mongol leader Tamerlane (aka Tamburlaine). Here's one Nasrudin tale which is still being told (in slightly different form) as a joke today:

Nasrudin is going across the border with a donkey carrying bundles of straw on its back. The border guard stops Nasrudin and asks him his business.

"I'm a smuggler!" Nasrudin replies bluntly.

The guard narrows his eyes. He searches through every single one of the bundles of straw that Nasrudin is taking across the border but he can't find anything and so has to let Nasrudin pass by.

The next day Nasrudin is back with his donkey laden with yet more bundles of straw. Again the border guard searches thoroughly through the straw. Again he cannot find anything and again he has to let Nasrudin pass by.

This pattern happens every day for several years during which time the guard begins to notice that Nasrudin is looking gradually wealthier and better dressed. Yet no matter how hard he searches, he cannot find what Nasrudin is smuggling.

Many years later when they are both old men, long after they have retired, the guard bumps into Nasrudin in the market place.

OK, Nasrudin," says the guard, "you can tell me now! Just what was it you were smuggling all those years?" "Donkeys!" says Nasrudin.

The Three Legged Dog In The Wild West Saloon

The doors are thrown open in a Wild West saloon. The pianist stops playing and everyone turns and looks. Framed in the door is a three-legged dog who walks in and says, "I'm looking for the man who shot my paw!"

The Pain In The Eye

A man goes to the doctor's and says,
"Doctor, I get a terrible pain in my eye every time I drink a cup of tea."
"Hm," says the doctor.
"Have you tried taking the teaspoon out of the cup first?"

Big Breaths

A doctor is examining a young
girl of admirable proportions.
He holds his stethoscope to
her chest and says,
"OK! Nice big breaths!"
"Yeth," replies the girl, "and
I'm only theventeen..."

The Man Whose Wife Made
Him A Millionaire

A man standing at a bar tells the
barman, "My wife made me a
millionaire." "Oh really?" says the
barman. "So what were you before?"
"A multi-millionaire," says the man.

You're Next!

A man gets home early from work and finds his wife in bed with his best friend. "Right! That's it!" he says pulling out a gun and pointing it to his own head. At this point his wife starts laughing hysterically. "I don't know what you're laughing for," says the man. "You're next!"

Two Men Doing A Crossword Puzzle

Two men are sitting doing a crossword puzzle. The first man reads a clue: "Old Macdonald had one. Four letters." "Farm!" says the second. "Very good," says the first. "How do you spell it?" The second thinks for a moment and then says definitively: "E-I-E-I-O!"

Taking The Cow To The Bull

Farmer Giles asks his youngest son to take their cow over to the bull at the farm on the other side of the village. A few minutes later the vicar sees the little boy struggling to lead the cow through the village. "Are you alright?" asks the vicar.

"Yes, vicar," says the little boy, "I'm taking the cow to the bull."

"Oh dear," says the vicar, concerned to see a small child in charge of such a large beast. "Couldn't your father help? Or can I do it instead?"

"Not really, vicar," says the little boy. "It has to be the bull."

The Three Tenders

The council want to build a monument in the town square so they put the job out to tender. Three tenders are received and the town clerk calls the three builders in for interview.

The first builder gives his tender of £3,000 and tells the clerk how it breaks down: "That's £1,000 for me, £1,000 for materials and £1,000 for my workmen."

"Very good," says the town clerk and calls in the next builder who gives a tender of £6,000.

"That's £2,000 for me," says the second builder, "£2,000 for materials and £2,000 for my workmen."

"Very good," says the town clerk and calls in the third builder who gives a tender of £9,000.

"That sounds a bit expensive," says the town clerk. "How does that break down?"

"Well," says the third builder, "it's £3,000 for me, £3,000 for you and then we give the job to the first builder!"

I Think I'm A Bridge

A man goes to the doctor and says, "Doctor, I keep thinking I'm a bridge." "My dear fellow," says the doctor, "what's come over you?" "So far this morning," says the man, "six cars, a tractor and a mini bus."

The Bump In The Carpet

A man is laying down a carpet for an old lady. When he has finished he decides to have a smoke but he cannot find his pack of cigarettes anywhere. Eventually he notices a small bulge in the otherwise flat carpet.

"Damn!" he says. "I've left my cigarettes under the carpet."

And so using a hammer he taps the lump until it is quite flat. Just at that moment the old lady walks in with a tray of tea things and the workman's cigarettes.

"You left these in the kitchen," says the old dear. "Now, you haven't seen my pet budgie anywhere have you?"

The Man Covered In Bandages

A man is lying in hospital covered from head to foot in bandages with two small slits for his eyes.

"What happened to you?" asks his friend.

"I was walking down the street," says the man, "when a lorry mounted the pavement and knocked me straight through a plate glass window."

"Oh no!" says his friend. "Still look on the bright side. If you hadn't been wearing all those bandages, you'd have been cut to pieces!"

The Political Speech

A man tells his friend that the previous night he had gone to see the local MP giving a speech which had lasted over an hour. "What was he talking about?" asks the friend.
"I don't know," says the man.
"He didn't say."

The Wooden Leg Christmas Present

A man tells his friend, "For Christmas this year, I bought my wife a wooden leg." "Oh really," says the friend. "Was that her main present?" "No," says the man. "It was just a stocking filler."

I Think I'm A Wigwam

A man goes to the doctor and says, "Doctor, sometimes I think I'm a wigwam and sometimes I think I'm a tepee." "I can tell you your problem," says the doctor. "You're two tents!"

Pornographic Pictures

A man is wandering around Soho when he is approached by a shifty looking individual. "Want to buy any pornographic pictures?" asks the shifty fellow. "Certainly not," says the man. "I don't even own a pornograph."

Dad's Youthful Indiscretions

A young boy goes to his father and says he wants to get married to Miss Green who lives in the next village.

"Oh no," says his dad, "you can't marry her. She's your half sister. When I was younger I had a bike and used to get around a bit."

"Oh dear," says the boy, "well in that case I think I'll marry Miss White instead."

"No," says dad. "You can't do that either. Miss White is also your half sister."

The boy now doesn't know what to do. He goes to his mother and tells her that his father has told him he can't marry Miss White or Miss Green because they are his half sisters.

"You marry whichever of them you like," says his mother. "He's not really your father!"

Antiques Roadshow

The Antiques Roadshow is in town. A man comes in dragging a huge metal box. "Where did you get this from?" asks the antiques expert. "Well," says the man. "I found it up in the attic. It's been there over 40 years. I think it's a bit of a family heirloom. Should I get insurance?" "Definitely you should," says the expert. "This is your water tank."

My Mother-In-Law
(according to Les Dawson and others)

My mother-in-law has come round
to our house at Christmas seven years
running. This year we're having a
change. We're going to let her in.

I asked the vet to cut off my dog's
tail. He said, "Why do you want to
do that?" I said, "My mother-in-law's
coming tomorrow and I don't want
her to think she's welcome."

My mother-in-law fell
down a wishing well, I was
amazed, I never knew they
worked.

My mother-in-law got run over yesterday. The driver said he would have gone round but he wasn't sure if he had enough petrol.

My mother-in-law had to stop skipping for exercise. It registered seven on the Richter scale.

The local peeping Tom knocked at my mother-in-law's last night. He asked her to close her blinds.

My mother-in-law has got so many chins it looks like she's staring at you over a sliced loaf.

My mother-in-law told me that when I die she would dance on my grave. I said, "Good. I'm being buried at sea."

19

Three New Recruits

Three new recruits for National Service are having their medical. The doctor walks up to the first, puts a stethoscope to his chest and listens to his heart beat.

"Marilyn Monroe," says the doctor. And the recruit's heart beat speeds up: "Bdum bdum bdum bdum bdum."
"Jayne Mansfield in the bath," says the doctor. The recruit's heartbeat speeds up even more: "Bdmbdmbdmbdmbdm."
"Thora Hird," says the doctor.
The recruit's heartbeat slows right down. "B-dummm b-dummmm b-dummmmm."

"OK," says the doctor. "Take your clothes off and go and stand behind that screen."

The next recruit steps up. "Marilyn

Monroe," says the doctor. "Bdum bdum bdum bdum bdum." "Jayne Mansfield in the bath." "Bdmbdmbdmbdmbdm." "Thora Hird". "B-dummm b-dummmm b-dummmm."

"OK. Take your clothes off and go stand behind the screen."

The final recruit steps up. "Marilyn Monroe," says the doctor. "B-dummm b-dummmm b-dummmm." "That's funny," says the doctor. "Jayne Mansfield in the bath." "B-dummm b-dummmm b-dummmm." The doctor is very confused. "Thora Hird," "B-dummm b-dummmm b-dummmm."

"OK. Never mind," says the doctor. "Take your clothes off and go and stand behind that screen with the other men."

"Bdmbdmbdbdmbm..."

Question and Answer Session

Q: What do you get if you drop
   a piano down a coal mine?
A: *A flat miner.*

Q: What do you get if you drop
   a piano on an army officer?
A: *A flat major.*

Q: What do you get if you dial 666?
A: *An upside down policeman.*

Q: What does a clock do when it's hungry?
A: *Goes back four seconds.*

Q: What did the policeman say to his stomach?
A: *You're under a vest.*

Q: Where did Napoleon keep his armies?
A: *Up his sleevies.*

Q: What cheese is made backwards?
A: *Edam.*

The Man With The Rich Elderly Father

A man proposes to a beautiful young girl and attempts to entice her by telling her that his father is 100 years old and possesses a fortune of several million pounds. The girl tells him to give her two weeks to think about it. Two weeks later he calls her to ask again if she will marry him and finds she has recently become his new stepmother.

Swinging The Guide Dog

A blind man walks into a shop and starts swinging his guide dog round and round on the end of its lead. "Can I help you, sir?" asks a shop assistant. "No, thank you," says the blind man. "I'm just having a look around."

Stop Biting Your Fingernails

A little boy is always biting his fingernails. His mother does everything she can to get him to stop. In the end she tells him, "Look! If you don't stop biting your fingernails, here's what will happen to you! Your fingernails will get stuck in your tummy and they will pile up inside you and make you go fatter and fatter until eventually you explode." Finally the message sinks in but a few days later the little boy is sitting on a bus when a heavily pregnant woman sits down opposite him. The little boy stares and stares at the pregnant woman's big round belly until in the end she asks sternly, "Do I know you?" "No," says the little boy, "but I know what you've been doing!"

Crossing The Road

Q: Why did the chicken cross the road?
A: To get to the other side.

Q: Why did the horse cross the road?
A: It was the chicken's day off.

Q: Why did the turkey cross the road?
A: To prove he wasn't chicken.

Q: Why did the giraffe cross the road?
A: To visit the chicken.

Q: Why did the dinosaur cross the road?
A: *Because chickens hadn't evolved yet.*

Q: Why did the cactus cross the road?
A: *It was stuck to the chicken's back.*

Q: Why did the dog cross the road?
A: *It was chasing the chicken.*

Q: Why did the cow cross the road?
A: *To get to the udder side.*

What Do You Call....

What do you call a man
covered in leaves?

Russell.

What do you call a man
with a plank on his head?
Edward.

What do you call a man with
a seagull on his head?
Cliff.

What do you call a man with
three planks on his head?
Edward Woodward.

What do you call a guy with
no arms and no legs who is
floating in the ocean?
Bob.

What do you call a man
with a bullet-proof head?
Helmut.

What do you call a man with
four planks on his head?
*I don't know, but Edward
Woodward would.*

The Amorous Milkman

A man tells his wife, "Apparently our milkman has made love to every woman in this street apart from one!" "I know!" says his wife. "I bet it's that stuck up cow at number 32!"

The Man Covered In Food

A man walks into the doctor's. He has a carrot in one ear, a banana in the other and a cucumber lodged up his nose. "Well, I can tell your problem," says the doctor. "You're not eating properly."

The Cost Of Getting Married

A little boy asks his daddy, "Daddy, how much does it cost to get married?" "I don't know, son," says dad. "I'm still paying."

The Irishman With Bottom Problems

An Irishman goes to the doctor complaining about a pain in his bottom. The doctor gets him to drop his trousers and examines him. "Incredible," says the doctor, "you seem to have a £20 note lodged up here." When the doctor removes the £20 note, he immediately finds another and then another and then another until he has accumulated a large amount of cash. "I've added it up," says the doctor, "and you had £1,980 stuffed up your backside." "Ah, that'll be it then, doctor," says the Irishman. "I knew I wasn't feeling two grand!"

Farmer Giles' Wife Gives Birth

Farmer Giles' wife is about to give birth. The doctor arrives but finds that amenities are very basic. Farmer Giles has no running water and no electricity. The doctor therefore has to ask for Giles' help while he delivers the baby.

"What you have to do," says the doctor, "is stand there holding this lantern. Ah, I think the baby's on the way!"

And after a few minutes the doctor is holding up the baby for Giles to admire.

"Congratulations, Giles," says the doctor, "you are the proud father of a fine strapping baby boy." But before Giles can say anything, the doctor says, "No, wait! Hold the lantern, Giles! I think there's another on the way!"

A few minutes later the doctor is holding up another baby for Giles to admire.

"Congratulations, Giles!" says the doctor. "You now not only have a fine strapping baby boy but also a beautiful baby daughter." But before Giles can say anything the doctor interrupts again: "No, wait! Hold the lantern, Giles! I think there's another on the way!"

A few minutes later the doctor is holding up yet another baby for Giles to admire.

Giles stands looking for a moment with his lantern in his hand and then says, "Doctor, do you think maybe it's the light that's attracting them?"

Elephants

Q: How can you tell if an elephant
has been in your fridge?
A: *Footprints in the butter.*

Q: How do you know if there's
an elephant in your bed?
A: *There's a big letter "E" on
the front of his pyjamas.*

Q: How many elephants can
you get in a Mini?
A: *Four: Two in the front,
two in the back.*

Q: How do you know there are four
   elephants in your refrigerator?
A: *There's an empty Mini parked
outside.*

Q: How do you know there
    are three elephants inside
    your refrigerator?
A: *You can't close the door.*

Q: How do you know there are two
   elephants in your refrigerator?
A: *You can hear giggling when the
   light goes out.*

Q: How many giraffes can you
   get in a Mini?
A: *None. It's full of elephants.*

35

The Rich Man And The Grass Eating Tramp

A rich man looks out of the window of his big house and sees a tramp down on all fours on the front lawn.

The rich man calls down, "What on earth are you doing?"

"I'm sorry, sir," says the tramp looking up at him. "But it's so long since I've eaten, I'm eating the grass in your front garden."

"Oh my dear fellow!" says the rich man. "Please! Don't do that! Just wait while I come down to you!"

The tramp waits while the rich man runs down the stairs and comes round to unlock the side gate.

"Here!" says the rich man. "Come through into the back garden. The grass is much longer there."

An Emergency Call From Old Mrs Riley's House

The phone rings at the police station and a panic stricken voice says, "Help, police! This is an emergency. You must come quick! A burglar has broken into old Mrs Riley's house and the old lady has managed to trap him in her bedroom."

"I see," says the policeman. "And who is this calling?"

"It's the burglar," says the voice.

Asking The Teacher For A Cigarette

A little boy asks his teacher, "Miss Thompson, can I have a cigarette?" "Certainly not," says the teacher. "Do you want to get me into trouble?" "If you like," says the boy. "But I'd rather have a cigarette."

The Mother-In-Law's Cremation

A man is at home with his mother-in-law one day when the mother-in-law suddenly announces, "I've decided I want to be cremated!" "No problem!" says the man. "Get your coat!"

The Tony Curtis Haircut

A man walks into a barber's and says, "I'd like my hair cut like Tony Curtis please."

"Certainly sir," says the barber, sitting the man down in the chair.

The barber begins snipping away while the man gets drowsy and falls asleep. When he wakes up he discovers his head is now untidily shaven with tufts sticking out in all directions.

"Hey! I asked you to cut my hair like Tony Curtis!" yells the man. "This isn't what Tony Curtis looks like."

"It would be if he came here!" says the barber.

I Think I'm A Chicken

A man goes to the doctor's and says, "Doctor, you've got to help me. I think I'm a chicken." "I see," says the doctor. "And how long as this been going on?" "Ever since I was an egg," says the man.

Phoning In Sick

The phone rings in the school office one morning. The secretary answers and a voice says, "I am phoning to let you know that little Jimmy is not well today and won't be able to come into school." "Oh dear," says the secretary. "Who is that speaking?" "This is my father," says the voice.

The Lost Rifle

A soldier in the army loses his rifle and has to report it. His commanding officer says, "That's all right. Hand me your pay book and we'll stop it out of your wages. It will cost you one thousand pounds." "Oh," says the soldier. "But what if I'd lost an armoured car?" "Then," says the officer, "we would stop the value of the armoured car from your pay." "Oh my goodness," says the soldier. "So that's why in the navy the captain always has to go down with his ship."

Jokes About Idiots

Insert the group or person of your choice in place of the word idiot

Did you hear about the idiot who was learning to tap dance?
He kept falling in the sink.

Did you hear about the idiot who couldn't complete a two piece jigsaw?
His excuse was that he had lost the lid.

Did you hear about the idiot who took a tie back to the shop?
He said it was too tight.

Did you hear about the idiot who fell
out of the window?
He had been trying to iron his curtains?

Did you hear about the idiot who
bought a pair of water skis?
Now he's looking for a lake with a slope.

Did you hear about the idiot
space mission to land on the sun?
*They went at night so it wouldn't
be too hot.*

**What's written at the top
of an idiot's step ladder?**
Stop here.

The Ink Blot Test

A man goes to a psychiatrist. The psychiatrist takes out a Rorschach ink blot test and says:

"I want you to look at this picture and tell me what you see."

The man looks carefully at the ink blot and says, "That's a man and a woman having sex on a bed."

"OK," says the psychiatrist and shows the man another ink blot.

"That's a man and a woman having sex on the beach," says the man.

The psychiatrist shows him a third ink blot and the man says, "And that's a man and a woman having sex in a park."

"Well," says the psychiatrist, " you seem to have an obsession with sex."

"What do you mean *I* have an obsession with sex!" says the man. "*You're* the one who keeps showing me dirty pictures!"

I Think I'm
A Deck Of Cards

A man goes into the
doctor's and says,
"Doctor, I think I'm
a deck of cards." "Sit
down there," says the
doctor, "I'll deal with
you later!"

A Horse Walks Into a Pub

"So," says the barman,
"why the long face?"

How Far To The Next Village

A man is walking through the country. He asks a local, "How far is it to the next village?" "Seven miles!" says the local. "But if you run you might do it in five."

The Pig With The Wooden Leg

A man is passing Farmer Giles's farmyard when he notices a pig with a wooden leg.

"I say," says the man, "why has your pig got a wooden leg?"

"Well," says the farmer, "he's a very special pig, that one. One night last year, the wife and me were asleep when that pig spotted the house was on fire. He broke down the door with his little piggy trotters, he ran up the stairs, he dragged me to safety. Then back in he went through the flames to fetch my wife. And then back in again he went to save the children. It's thanks to that pig, we're all still here today."

"I see," says the man, "so he hurt his leg in the fire, did he?"

"Oh no," says Farmer Giles. "But, you see, when you've got a pig as special as this one, you don't want to eat it all at once."

Question and Answer Session

Q: Why was the mushroom invited to the party?

A: *Because he was a fun-guy.*

Q: What time does the Chinese dentist's open?

A: *Tooth hurtee.*

Q: Why are there no aspirins in the jungle?

A: *Because the parrots eat 'em all.*

Q: What's black and white
   and read all over?
A: *A newspaper.*

Q: What is black and white
   and eats like a horse?
A: *A zebra.*

Q: What's black and white and
   goes round and round?
A: *A penguin in a revolving door.*

Q: What's black and white
   and red all over?
A: *A penguin with sunburn.*

47

Fish and Chips Twice

A man walks into a chip shop and calls out, "Fish and chips twice!" "OK!" says the owner. "I heard you the first time."

The Less Than Proficient Shave

A man goes into a barber's for a shave. The barber turns out to be less than proficient with the razor and nicks the man all over his face. After the shave the man asks for a glass of water. "Are you thirsty?" asks the barber. "No," says the man. "I just want to see if my face leaks."

I Think I'm A Snooker Ball

A man goes in to the doctor's and says, "Doctor, I think I'm a snooker ball." "I'm sorry," says the doctor. "You'll have to get to the end of the cue."

The Not At All Well Squid

A shark is swimming in the ocean when he bumps into a squid.

"Please don't eat me, Mr Shark," says the squid, "I'm not feeling very good today. I've been spending too much time at the bottom of the ocean and now I feel very poorly."

"Oh dear," says the shark. "Tell you what. Jump on my back and I'll take you back up to the top."

So the squid climbs on the shark's back and the shark swims him back to the top of the ocean where they meet a killer whale.

"Hello," says the killer whale to the shark. "What have you got there?"

"Hey, Fred," replies the shark. "I've brought you that sick squid I owe you!"

The Guide Chihuahua

A man walks into a pub with a little Chihuahua on a lead. The landlord tells him, "Sorry, sir. No dogs allowed in here." "But," says the man, "I thought you allowed guide dogs." "Yes," says the landlord, "but guide dogs tend to be German Shepherds or Labradors." "Oh no," says the man. "What have they given me this time?"

Have You Heard
The Joke About…

Have you heard the joke
about the bed?
*Well, you can't because it
hasn't been made yet.*

Have you heard the joke
about the pencil?
There's no point to it.

Have you heard the joke
about the butter?
*I'd tell you but I know you'd
only spread it around.*

Have you heard the joke
about the old man's foot?
It's too corny.

Have you heard the
joke about the dustbin?
It's rubbish.

                        Have you heard the
                        joke about the drill?
                        It's boring.

Have you heard the joke
about the glass door?
I couldn't see it myself.

                    **Have you heard the joke about
                    the letter lost in the post?
                    *To be honest, I didn't get it.***

Have heard the joke about
my willy?
It's a bit too long really.

Farmer Giles' Son And The Muck Pile

A man is walking through the country and comes across a farm truck which has shed its load over the lane. The man notices a small boy dripping with sweat while frantically shovelling the enormous pile of horse manure back onto the truck.

"Are you alright there, young fellow?" asks the man. "Why not stop for a moment?"

"No," says the boy. "I can't stop. Dad wouldn't like it."

"But," says the man, "that's such a huge pile of muck for a small boy to shovel. I think you should sit down and have a rest."

"No," says the boy, "I can't stop. Dad wouldn't like it."

"Well," says the man, "at least have a sip of my bottle of water."

"No," says the boy, "I can't stop. Dad wouldn't like it."

"I must say," says the man, "your dad sounds like a bit of a slave driver. I think I ought to have a word with him. Where can I find him?"

"He's underneath this pile of horse manure!" says the boy.

I Think I'm A Pair Of Curtains

A man goes into the doctor's and says, "Doctor, I think I'm a pair of curtains." "Pull yourself together, man!" says the doctor.

Destroying The German Lines of Communication

A man tells a friend, "My father was a solider in the First World War. He single handedly destroyed the German lines of communication."

"What did he do?" asks the friend.

"He ate their pigeon," says the man.

The Monk And The Vow Of Silence

A man goes to become a monk. He enters the monastery and the abbot tells him, "Here we have a strict vow of silence. You are only allowed to say two words every seven years."

The man agrees to take the vow. After seven years, he goes to see the abbot who indicates he may say his two words.

"Food cold!" says the man.

The abbot nods. Another seven years passes by. The man is again invited by the abbot to say his two words.

"Robe dirty," he says.

The abbot nods and another seven years passes by. Again the man comes in to see the abbot who indicates he may say his two words.

"I quit!" says the man.

"Well," says the abbot. "quite frankly I'm not surprised. You've done nothing but complain since you got here!"

Waiter!

"Waiter, there's a fly in my soup."
"Keep it down, sir, or everyone will
want one."

"Waiter, what's this fly doing
in my soup?"
"It appears to be the breast
stroke, sir."

"Waiter, your thumb is in my soup."
"Don't worry, sir. It's not hot."

"Waiter, what is this?"
"It's bean soup."
"I don't care what it's been, what is it now?"

"Waiter, there's a live fly in my soup."
"Don't worry, sir. He won't survive
long in that stuff."

"Waiter, there's a fly in my soup."
"Don't worry, sir. The spider on your bread will soon get him."

"Waiter, this coffee tastes like dirt."
"That's because it was fresh ground this morning."

"Waiter, will my burger be long?"
"No, sir. It will be round."

"Waiter, there's a fly swimming in my soup."
"Look on the bright side. If the portions weren't so generous, he'd be wading."

Fish And Chips
In The Library

An man goes into a library and says, "A portion of fish and chips please!" The librarian says, "Don't you realize this is a library?" "Sorry," says the man and then whispers very quietly, "A portion of fish and chips please!"

The Bald Man At The Barber's

An extremely bald man goes to the barber's for a trim.

When the barber is finished he tells the man that the charge is £10.

"Ten pounds!" exclaims the man. "How can you charge that much when I had practically no hair to begin with?"

"Well you see, sir," says the barber, "it's one pound for cutting your hair and nine pounds for the search fee."

Flight Delay

A man is sitting on a plane that has been waiting to take off for two hours. He calls over to the stewardess to ask why the flight is delayed. "I'm sorry, sir," says the stewardess. "The pilot has heard a funny noise from the engine that he doesn't like." "Oh," says the man, "so you're waiting for an engineer to come and fix the problem?" "No," says the stewardess, "we're waiting for another pilot who can't hear it."

The Musical Octopus

A sailor walks into a harbour bar with his pet octopus next to him.

He announces to the astonished drinkers, "I bet any of you £50 that my octopus here can play any musical instrument it is given."

The people in the bar look around and someone produces an old concertina. The octopus has a look, picks it up and starts squeezing out a burst of "What shall we do with the drunken sailor."

Another patron steps up with a trumpet. The octopus takes it, loosens up the keys, licks its beaky mouth and starts playing "Land of Hope and Glory."

The bar owner then disappears into the back room and returns with a set of bagpipes.

"Double or quits says your octopus can't play these," says the bar owner.

The octopus examines the bagpipes, lifts them up, turns them over and has another look from a different angle.

Puzzled, the sailor whispers to the octopus, "What are you messing around for? Hurry up and play a tune on this thing or we'll lose the bet."

"What do you mean play a tune on it?" says the octopus. "As soon as I work out how to get its knickers off I'm going to have my evil way with it!"

Did You Hear About…

Did you hear about the man who
fell into the lens-grinding machine?
He made a spectacle of himself.

Did you hear about the
man with five penises?
*His underpants fitted him
like a glove.*

Did you hear about
the dyslexic atheist?
*He didn't believe there
was a dog.*

Did you hear about the
one-fingered pickpocket?
*He specializes in stealing
Polo mints.*

Did you hear about
the Jewish detective?
He had a tip off.

Did you hear about the
dyslexic devil worshipper?
He sold his soul to Santa.

Did you hear about the
short-sighted rabbi?
He got the sack.

The Furry Lemon

A barman says to his wife,
"Blimey! I think these lemons
we've got on the bar have gone off.
The last one I picked up felt quite
furry." "You idiot," says his wife,
"you've just squeezed my budgie
into that bloke's drink."

The Mother-in-law On Holiday

A man goes on holiday to Africa
with his wife and her mother.
A lion leaps out of the jungle
and corners her. The man's wife
says, "Aren't you going to help?"
"No," says the man. "The lion got
himself into this mess, he can get
himself out of it."

I've Swallowed A Watch

A man goes into the doctor's and says, "Doctor, I've swallowed a watch. What should I do?" "Take these pills," says the doctor. "They should help you pass the time."

Liver Salts

An old man drinks liver salts every day for 50 years. He dies on Monday, is buried on Wednesday and on Friday the mourners have to go back to the cemetery to beat his liver to death with a stick.

Question and Answer Session

Q: What's round, brown and skims
   across a lake at 30 mph?
A: *A digestive biscuit with an
   outboard motor*

Q: Who's the coolest person
   in the hospital?
A: *The ultra-sound guy.*

Q: What's the similarity
   between the *USS Enterprise*
   and a piece of toilet paper?
A: *They both circle Uranus on
   a mission to wipe out the
   Klingons.*

Q: Why do bagpipe players
march as they play?
A: *They're trying to get
away from the noise.*

Q: What do Eskimos get from
sitting on a the ice for too long?
A: *Polaroids.*

Q: What do John the Baptist and
Winnie the Pooh have in common?
A: *They have the same middle name.*

Q: What kind of pizza does
Good King Wenceslas like?
A: *A deep pan, crisp and even.*

German Jokes

It is often said the Germans have no sense of humour but how can anyone say such things of the nation which came up with the following rib ticklers:

Yesterday, I met my friend Horst at the hospital. He'd swallowed a sponge. He says it doesn't hurt but he's always thirsty.

Three little German boys are arguing about whose father is the fastest. The first says: "My daddy is a racing driver so he is the fastest." The second says, "No. My daddy is a pilot in the Luftwaffe so he is even faster." "That's nothing," says the third. "My father is a state official. He is so fast that if work finishes at 5pm, he gets home 4 hours earlier."

What would you do if the world was about to end? Go to East Friesland. Everything happens 50 years later there.

What does an Opel Manta driver say to a tree after crashing into it? "Why didn't you get out of my way? I used the horn!"

A German is on holiday in New York. He walks into a McDonald's and orders a beer. A New Yorker standing behind him in the queue, laughs and says, "You German idiot! They don't serve beer here!" The German turns and says, "Let me get this straight, you've come in here just for the food and you're calling <u>me</u> the idiot!"

The Elderly Couple's Plane Ride

The pilot of a light aircraft is at an air show where he is offering trips in his plane for £25 per person.

During the afternoon the pilot hears an elderly couple bickering nearby. The old lady has never been in a plane in her life and wants to go up for a flight. Her husband however thinks that £25 each is too expensive for them.

In order to stop the incessant noise of the argument the pilot decides to make them an offer.

"I'll tell you what," he says. "I'll take you up in the plane for £25 for both of you. There's one condition though. You have to stop this terrible arguing. If I hear either of you say a word while we're up in the air, you'll have to pay the full price."

The elderly couple are delighted by the offer. They climb into the plane, the pilot takes them up and gives them the ride of their lives.

He twists and turns and rolls and dives and loops the loop and the couple, true to their word, don't say a thing.

When they get down, the pilot says, "That's amazing. I did all the tricks I could up there but you didn't say a word."

"Well, to be honest," says the old man, "I was going to say something when my wife fell out of the plane, but £25 is £25."

Cough Treatment

A chemist comes back after lunch and notices a man leaning against the shop wall. "He came in for some cough syrup," explains the assistant, "but we didn't have any in stock so I had to give him a powerful laxative instead." "What good is that going to do?" asks the chemist. "Giving him a laxative isn't going to stop him coughing." "Well, it has," says the assistant. "He's too frightened to cough now."

The Maid Is Given Notice

A lady gives her maid notice so the maid decides to tell her exactly what she thinks. "You might like to know," says the maid, "that I am a better housekeeper than you are, I am a better cook, I am better company and I am much more attractive." "Really!" says the lady. "And who told you that?" "Your husband!" says the maid. "And also I'm much better than you are in bed." "What!" says the lady aghast. "My husband told you that as well?!" "No," says the maid. "The gardener did."

The Wasp Shop

A man walks into a shop and says, "I'd like to buy a wasp please." "I'm sorry, sir," says the shopkeeper, "but we don't sell wasps." "Really?" says the man. "You've got one in the window!"

Carrier Pigeon Message

During the First World War a platoon of soldiers are under bombardment from the Germans while waiting in a trench for orders sent by carrier pigeon. They see the pigeon flying towards them with a message but then suddenly the bird falls from the sky.

The Captain asks for a volunteer to go out into no-man's land to get the message from the pigeon. One brave soldier volunteers. He climbs over the top and runs out into no-man's land. His comrades hear a continual barrage of gunfire and bombs going off and have to conclude that he will not return.

Two hours later however they are surprised to see him climbing back into the trench covered in dirt, blood and soot.

The men give him three cheers for his safe return and the captain steps forward.

"So did you find the pigeon?" asks the captain.

"Yes I did, sir," says the soldier.

"And did the pigeon have a message?" asks the captain.

"Yes it did, sir," says the soldier.

"And what was the message?" asks the captain.

"Coooooo!" says the soldier. "Coooooooo!"

The Woman With Four Husbands

A woman tells a friend that she is getting married for the fourth time. "How marvellous!" exclaims her friend. "But, I hope you don't mind me asking, what happened to your first husband?" "He ate poisonous mushrooms and died," says the woman. "Oh dear," says the friend. "And what about your second husband?" "He also ate poisonous mushrooms and died," says the woman. "That's very unlucky," says the friend. "But surely the same thing can't have happened to your third husband." "No, he died of a broken neck." "Oh dear. How did that happen?" "He wouldn't eat the mushrooms."

Where Were You Born?

A man is being interviewed. "Where were you born?" asks the interviewer. "London," says the man. "Oh yes," says the interviewer. "Which part?" "All of me," says the man.

The Horse Breaks Wind

The bishop goes to visit a vicar who meets him from the station in his horse and trap. As they are going home through the village the horse suddenly and very noisily breaks wind. "I'm terribly sorry about that," says the vicar, very embarrassed. "Don't mention it," says the bishop. "To be honest, if you hadn't said anything I'd have thought it was the horse."

Skoda Jokes

Q: How do you double the
value of a Skoda?
A: *Fill it with petrol.*

Q: **Why do Skodas have
heated rear windows?**
A: *To keep your hands warm
while you're pushing it.*

Q: How do you make a
Skoda disappear?
A: *Apply rust remover.*

Q: What do you call a Skoda
with twin exhausts?
A: *A wheelbarrow.*

Q: What information do you
get in every Skoda log book?
A: *A bus timetable.*

Q: What do you call a
Skoda at the top of a hill?
A: *A miracle.*

Q: What do you call a
Skoda with a flat tyre?
A: *A write-off.*

The Stolen Credit Card

A man says to his friend, "My wife's credit card was stolen last week." "Have you reported it to the police?" asks his friend. "No," says the man. "I just got the statement this morning. At the moment the thief is spending less than my wife."

The Ugly Baby On The Bus

A woman gets on a bus carrying her baby. The driver says, "Blimey! That's the ugliest baby I've ever seen." The woman goes to her seat absolutely fuming. "What's the matter?" asks the man sitting next to her. "That bus driver was extremely rude to me," says the woman. "Oh you shouldn't put up with that," says the man. "You go and tell him off. Here! I'll hold your monkey for you."

Entering The Olympics

An Englishman, a Scotsman and an Irishman are trying to get into the Olympic Games but don't have tickets. They try to think up ideas for how to bluff their way past the ticket clerk. In the end the Scotsman marches in with a large stick and says, "Scotland! Javelin!" And the ticket clerk lets him in. Next the Englishman marches up carrying a bin lid and says, "England! Discus!" And the ticket clerk lets him in. Finally the Irishman marches up with a roll of chicken wire and some posts and says, "Ireland! Fencing!"

I Think I'm A Bell

A man goes to the doctor's and
says, "Doctor, I think I'm a bell."
"Take these pills," says the
doctor, "and if they don't work,
give me a ring."

Two Unexploded Bombs

Two navvies are working on a building site when they
dig up an unexploded bomb from the war. "Blimey!
What do you think we should do with this," asks
one. "Let's put it on the wheelbarrow," says the other.
"Then we can take it along to the foreman later." A
bit later on the pair dig up another bomb. They put
it in the wheelbarrow next to the first and are just
wheeling them along to the foreman's office when
they notice the second bomb has started ticking. "Oh
no!" says the first. "What will we do if this second
bomb blows up?" "Don't worry," says the other.
"We'll tell the foreman we only found one."

Operated On Just In Time

A man is telling his friend about his nephew.
"They rushed him into hospital and they only just
managed to operate on him in time," says the man.
"Really?" says the friend. "Yes," says the man. "One
more day and he would have got better on his own."

Three Old Men And Their Toiletary Problems

Three old men are talking.

"I have terrible problems," says the first old man. "I feel like I need to wee all the time but when I stand at the toilet I can't make myself go."

"You think you've got problems," says the second. "No matter what I take I am constipated all the time and cannot move my bowels."

"You think you two have got problems," says the third old man. "Every morning at 7 o'clock I wee like a carthorse. Then every morning at 8 o'clock on the dot I have the most extraordinarily thorough bowel movement."

"What's the matter with that?" say the other two. "You wee at 7, you have a bowel movement at 8. It sounds like everything's working perfectly."

"Yes but there's just one problem," says the third old man. "I don't get out of bed till 9."

The Lottery Winners

A man and his wife win a huge prize on the lottery. "What shall we do about the begging letters?" asks the wife. "That's OK," says the man, "we'll just keep sending them."

Twenty Four Hours To Live

A man is in hospital and the doctor tells him, "we've had your test results back and I've got good news and bad news." "OK," says the man. "What's the good news?" "Your tests show you've got 24 hours to live." "Oh," says the man. "So what's the bad news?" "I was supposed to tell you this yesterday," says the doctor.

Two Lions In The Middle Of London

Two lions are wandering through the centre of London. One says to the other: "Not many people around today, are there?"

Two Men Doing A Crossword Puzzle

Two men are sitting doing a crossword puzzle. The first man reads a clue: "What was Gandhi's first name?" "Was it Goosey Goosey?" suggests the second.

The Identity Parade

A woman goes to the police station and reports that a man has just exposed himself to her. A group of men are lined up for the identity parade. The woman is then brought in, at which point the man at the end of the line-up steps forward and says, "Yes, officer. That's her!"

The Travels Of Various People's Wives

"My wife's just gone to the West Indies."
"*Jamaica?*"
"No, she went of her own accord."

"I just took my wife on holiday to Indonesia."
"*Jakarta?*"
"No, we went by plane."

"My wife's gone to northern Italy."
"*Genoa?*"
"Of course I do. We've been married 20 years."

"My wife's just been for a holiday in Poole."
"*In Dorset?*"
"Oh yes, she thoroughly recommends it."

"I've just taken my wife for a romantic weekend in north Wales."
"Bangor?"
"I say! That's a rather personal question."

"My wife fell over climbing up the side of a volcano in Indonesia."
"Krakatoa?"
"No, she broke her whole leg actually."

"Where's your wife going on holiday this year?"
"Alaska."
"No, don't bother her. I just thought you'd know."

"My wife's just gone to the south east of England."
"Surrey?"
"I SAID MY WIFE'S JUST GONE TO THE SOUTH EAST OF ENGLAND!

Jokes About Idiots

Insert the group or person of your choice in place of the word idiot

Did you hear about the idiot's toilet roll?
It has instructions printed on each sheet.

Did you hear about the idiot's beer bottle?
It has "open other end" written on the bottom.

Did you hear about the idiot who tried to row the Atlantic single handed?
He couldn't understand why he kept going round in circles.

Did you hear about the
idiot kidnappers?
*They sent the hostage home
with the ransom note.*

Did you hear about the two idiots
who went into a restaurant?
*They ordered a meal and then
sneaked out without eating it.*

Did you hear about the idiot who
climbed on the pub roof?
*The landlord had told him the
drinks were on the house.*

Advice For The Overweight

A woman is suffering from obesity. Her doctor puts her on a diet to help her lose weight. The doctor tells her, "What I want you to do is have your meals as normal for two days, then I want you to skip a day. Then you eat normally for another two days, then skip another day and so on. That way you should lose five pounds in the next two weeks." Two weeks later, the woman comes back. She has lost 4 stone. "That's amazing," says the doctor. "Did you follow my instructions?" "Yes," says the woman. "I thought I was going to die on the third day." "From the hunger?" asks the doctor. "No," says the woman. "From all the skipping!"

Animal Biscuits

A man tells his friend, "I bought a box of those animal biscuits." "Were they nice?" asks his friend. "I didn't get to try them," says the man. "It said on the box 'Do not eat if seal is broken' and when I looked inside, would you believe it…!"

The Swedish Chemist's

A man walks into a Swedish chemist's and says, "I would like to buy a deodorant please." "Certainly, sir," says the chemist. "Ball or aerosol?" "Neither," says the man. "I want it for under my armpits.

Constant Emissions

A man goes to his doctor suffering from constant gas emissions. "Right," says the doctor, "drop your trousers and let's have a look." The doctor gets out a six-foot long wooden pole. "What are you doing?" asks the man nervously. "Well," says the doctor, "before I examine you I think I'd better just open the window."

Examining A Cow

Farmer Giles takes his son to buy a cow. Giles gives the cow a thorough examination prodding and feeling the animal all over and lifting its tail to check every nook and cranny. "Why are you doing that, daddy?" asks his son. "Well," says Farmer Giles, "before you pay good money you have to give the animal a going over." The next morning the lad runs up and says, "Dad! I just saw mummy and the postman behind the barn. And do you know what? I think he might be considering buying her!"

The Man With A Pancake On His Head

A man walks into a psychiatrist's office with a pancake on his head, a fried egg on each shoulder and a rasher of bacon over each ear. "OK," says the psychiatrist, "what seems to be the problem?" "I'm worried about my brother," says the man.

Phoning Home From The Office

A man phones home from the office and hears a strange woman's voice answer. "Who's that?" he asks.

"This is the maid," says the woman.

"But I don't have a maid," says the man.

"But I was just hired this morning," says the woman, "by the lady of the house."

"Well," says the man, "this is her husband speaking. Is she there?"

"Oh," says the woman, "she's upstairs at the moment with another gentleman who I assumed was her husband."

"What the hell is going on there!" says the man fuming. "OK. I will pay you £50,000. Go to my desk, in the top drawer you will find a loaded revolver. Take it. Go up to the bedroom. Shoot the pair of them. I will take full responsibility."

"Yes, sir," says the woman. The man then hears footsteps going up the stairs, a couple of gunshots and then the footsteps returning.

"Right," says the woman, "what would you like me to do with the bodies? "

"Throw them in the swimming pool!" says the man.

"But," says the woman, "there isn't a swimming pool here."

"Oh!" says the man. "This is 632 4821 isn't it?"

Question and Answer Session

Q: What did one eye say to
the other?

A: *Between you and me,
something smells.*

Q: What did the traffic
light say to the car?

A: *Don't look now, I'm
changing.*

Q: What did the scarf say to the hat?

A: *You go on ahead, I'll hang around.*

Q: What did the envelope
say to the stamp?
A: *Stick with me, baby,
and we'll go places.*

Q: What did the big chimney
say to the little chimney?
A: *You're too young to smoke.*

Q: What did one wall say to
the other wall?
A: *Meet me at the corner.*

Q: What did Big Ben say to the
Leaning Tower of Pisa?
A: *I've got the time if you've
got the inclination!*

The Grumpy Bald Man With The Wooden Leg

A man with a big bald head and a wooden leg receives an invitation to a fancy dress party. He doesn't know what to wear so he writes to a mail order fancy dress company to ask if they have any costumes that will hide both his bald head and his wooden leg.

The company send him a package in return with a note which says:

"'Dear Sir, please find herewith a pirate's outfit. The bandana will cover your bald head and your wooden leg will fit in perfectly with the pirate theme."

The man is however furious and writes back to complain that the company has sent him a costume which emphasises his disability.

A few days later he receives another package with a note which says:

"Dear Sir, please accept out apologies for the costume you were previously sent. Instead please find herewith a monk's habit. The habit will hide your wooden leg and your bald head will fit in perfectly with the monk-ish theme."

Again the man is furious and writes to complain that the fancy dress company have sent him a costume that this time draws attention to his bald head.

A few days later he receives another consignment with a note:

"Dear Sir, please find enclosed a tin of treacle. We suggest you open the tin, hold it over your head, pour the contents over your bald bonce, stand on your wooden leg and go to the party as a toffee apple, you grumpy old sod!"

Two Mexicans Starving In The Desert

Two Mexicans are lost and starving in the desert. In the distance they see a tree. As they approach they see juicy rashers of bacon are hanging from every branch. "Hey, Pepe," says the first Mexican. "Eez a bacon tree. We are saved, amigo!" But just as he approaches the tree, shots ring out and he falls to the ground. Pepe runs to help his friend. "Quick, amigo! Save yourself!" says the first Mexican. "This eez not a bacon tree after all. Eez a ham bush!"

The Rag and Bone Man Collecting Bottles

A rag and bone man knocks on a woman's front door. A stern-looking woman answers and the rag and bone man asks her if she has any beer bottles. She is appalled. She says, "Do I look like the sort of person that drinks beer?" "Sorry," says the rag and bone man. "So do you have any vinegar bottles?"

Two Men In The Jungle

Two men are walking through the jungle. One of them picks up a huge stick and throws it into the forest where it whacks a lion on the head and wakes the beast up. "Oh no!" says the first man. "Looks like we better run for our lives!" "I'm not running!" says the second. "You're the one who threw the stick!"

Wife Like A Peach

Two men are talking. One says to the other, "My wife is like a peach." "Ah," says the second. "That's nice. You mean because she's nice and sweet and soft." "No," says the first. "Because she's got a heart of stone."

Couple Not Talking

Two men are talking. One says to the other, "I haven't spoken to my wife for 15 years." "Why's that?" asks the second. "I don't like to interrupt," says the first.

Talking While Making Love

Two women are talking. One says to the other, "Do you ever talk to your husband while making love?" "Not really," says the second. "Only if he phones me up."

Widow Jones

A man is dragging a large box up the driveway to a house. He knocks on the door and a woman answers. "Hello," says the man. "Are you Widow Jones?" "No," says the woman. "My name is not Widow Jones. I am Mrs Jones." "Hang on," says the man, "you haven't seen what's in this box yet."

The Man Converted To Religion By His Wife

A man tells his friend, "My wife converted me to religion. Before I married her I didn't believe in hell."

The Firing Squad

Three men are due to be executed by firing squad. The first man steps up and as the firing squad raise their guns, he shouts, "Tornado!" The firing squad all turn to look and the man takes his chance, runs off and escapes. The second man steps up. Again just as the firing squad are raising their guns, he shouts, "Earthquake!" The firing squad all turn to look and the second man escapes. Finally the third man is led before the firing squad and thinks he will try the same trick. The firing squad raise their guns but just as they do so, the third man shouts, "Fire!"

Two Workmen Digging A Hole

Two men are working in the park. A passer-by notices them and watches what they are doing. One of the men digs a hole, then the other fills it in. They keep moving along the side of the path, doing the same thing each time. "Excuse me," says the passer-by. "What exactly are you doing?" "Well," says one of the men. "There's usually three of us. I dig the hole. Fred plants a tree and Stan fills the hole in again." "But," says the passer-by, "you aren't planting any trees." "I know," says the man. "Fred's off sick. But that doesn't mean me and Stan have to lose a day's work does it?"

Cannibals

Did you hear about the cannibal
who passed his mother-in-law in
the woods?

One cannibal says to another, "I don't
like my mother-in-law." "Well then,"
says his friend, "just eat the chips."

One cannibal says to another,
"What's for dinner?" "Shut up,"
says his friend, "and get back in
the oven."

Two cannibals are eating a clown.
One says to the other, "Does this
taste funny to you?"

**Did you hear about the cannibal
who went on a self catering holiday?
He had to eat himself.**

Two cannibals are having
dinner. One says to the other,
"Your wife makes great soup."
"Yes," says the other, "but I'm
still going to miss her."

**Did you hear about the cannibal
who tried to commit suicide?
He got himself into a right stew.**

Two lady cannibals are talking.
One says to the other, "I don't
know what to make of my
husband these days." "How about
a curry," says her friend.

Did You Hear About...

Did you hear about the cat that swallowed a ball of wool?
It had mittens.

Did you hear about the constipated accountant?
He just couldn't budget.

Did you hear about the dyslexic pimp?
He bought a warehouse.

Did you hear about the cowboy
covered in brown paper?
He was arrested for rustling.

Did you hear about the farmer
who won the Nobel Prize?
*They said he was outstanding in
his field.*

Did you hear about the
man who lost his left
arm and left leg in a car
accident?
He's all right now.

**Did you hear that Old MacDonald
was dyslexic?**
O-I-E-O-I!

I Keep Forgetting Things

A man goes into the doctor's and says, "Doctor, I keep forgetting things." "How long has this been going on?" asks the doctor. "How long has what been going on?" asks the man.

The Little Boy Caught Cheating

A teacher says to one of her pupils, "I know you were copying your answers in the test today off the boy sitting next to you." "How can you tell that?" asks the pupil. "Easy," says the teacher. "When he gave the answer 'I don't know' for question 10, you wrote 'Neither do I'."

Which Day Is Your Birthday

A man is being interviewed. "When is your birthday?" asks the interviewer. "November the twelfth," says the man. "Which year?" asks the interviewer. "Every year," says the man.

Colour Blind

A man is having his eyes tested. The optician tells him, "I've got news for you. It turns out that you are colour blind." "Oh my goodness!" says the man. "Well, that's certainly a bolt out of the green!"

The Prisoner's Laundry

A man comes out of prison after having been inside for five years. He is given his suit as he leaves and when he checks his breast pocket he discovers a wrinkled old laundry ticket. He finds his way to the cleaners, goes inside, presents his ticket and is told, "It'll be ready on Friday."

The Goldfish With Epilepsy

A man takes his goldfish to the vet. "What's the problem?" asks the vet. "I think he might have epilepsy," says the man. "He looks all right to me," says the vet. "Ah," says the man. "But you haven't seen him out of the bowl."

My Mother-In-Law

I've just got back from a pleasure trip. I was taking the wife's mother to the airport.

I can always tell when the mother-in-law's coming to stay; the mice start throwing themselves on the traps.

My wife asked me, "Can my mother come down for the weekend?" I asked why. "Well," she said, "she's been up on the roof two weeks now."

My mother was very house proud. She divorced her first husband because he clashed with the curtains.

What's the punishment for bigamy?
Two mothers-in-law.

What's the definition of
mixed emotions? Seeing your
mother-in-law backing over a
cliff in your car.

My mother-in-law had to
stop skipping for exercise.
It registered seven on the
Richter scale.

It's surely no coincidence that
mother-in-law is an anagram
of "Woman Hitler".

The Death of Robin Hood

Robin Hood lies dying and summons Maid Marian, Little John and the rest of the Merry Men to his bedside. He raises his head and says quietly to them, "Bring me my bow and an arrow true, that I may loose a final shaft. And wheresoever that shaft may find its rest, bury this poor body there." Then commending his soul to the almighty he draws his bow and lets fly his final shot. And so three days later, true to Robin's last request, they bury him on top of the wardrobe.

Noddy Holder Goes Back On Tour

Noddy Holder is going back on tour with Slade so he goes to a trendy boutique to get himself kitted out. He walks up to the counter and asks for a pair of gold lamé loon pants, a pair of platformed boots and a mirrored top hat. "Certainly, sir," says the assistant, "and what about a kipper tie as well?" "Oh ta!" says Noddy. "Milk and two sugars in mine!"

The Salesman At The Door

A travelling salesman knocks at a door. A little boy answers. The little boy is smoking a huge cigar, swigging from a bottle of whisky and standing with his arm round a busty young woman. The salesman looks at him and asks, "Are your mother and father at home?" "Does it look like they are?" says the boy.

Assassin Assessment

Three men have applied to the Secret Service for the post of assassin and have to undergo an aptitude test. The interviewer shows the first candidate a locked door, hands him a revolver and tells him, "We must be sure that you will follow instructions, no matter what. Inside this room, you will find your wife sitting in a chair. I want you to go in and shoot her with this revolver!"

"No!" says the man, "I could never do such a thing!"

"Then," says the interviewer showing him the door, "we have no place for you in the Secret Service!"

The second candidate is brought in and given the same instructions. He takes the revolver, goes into the room but after a few minutes emerges with tears in his eyes. "It's no good," he sobs, "I just couldn't do it. I could never shoot my own wife!"

"Then," says the interviewer, "we have no place for you in the Secret Service either!"

The final candidate is brought in and handed the revolver. He walks into the room and closes the door behind him. The instructor then hears a series of clicks from inside the room followed by the sound of screaming, crashing and banging. Finally the candidate emerges wiping sweat from his brow.

"What happened?" asks the interviewer.

"That gun you gave me turned out not to be loaded!" says the candidate. "In the end I had to beat her to death with the chair."

Question and Answer Session

Q: What's worse than finding
   a worm in an apple?
A: *Finding half a worm.*

Q: **Why do giraffes have
   such long necks?**
A: *Their feet smell.*

Q: Why do birds fly South
   in the winter?
A: *It's too far to walk.*

108

Q: Why do cows have bells?
A: *Because their horns don't work.*

Q: What did the monkey say
when he fell out of the tree?
A: *Oooh oooh aaah aaah!*

Q: What goes "Zzub
zzzub zzub zzub"?
A: *A bee flying backwards.*

Getting One Over On The Cannibals

Two men get caught by cannibals. The cannibals put them in a huge pot, cover them with gravy, light a huge fire underneath them and leave them to stew. A few minutes later, one of the men begins laughing hysterically. "I can't believe it!" says his friend. "This is as bad as it gets and yet you find it funny! We're being boiled alive and then the cannibals are going to eat us!" "I know," says the second, "but I've just weed in their gravy!"

Aspirin Overdose

A man tells his friend, "I was feeling so depressed the other day I decided to commit suicide by taking an overdose of aspirin." "Oh dear," says his friend. "So what happened?" "Well," says the man, "after I'd taken a couple I began to feel a bit better."

Fighting Off The Muggers

A man is jumped by two muggers. The muggers try to pin him down but he fights like a wildcat. In the end it takes half an hour of tussling for them to overpower him and take out his wallet. Inside they find just 57 pence. "What the hell is this?!" says one of the muggers. "You fought like that for just 57p?!" "Of course not," says the man. "I thought you were after the two hundred quid I've got hidden in my shoe!"

The Little German Boy

A couple have a baby son. After the doctor has checked the child he informs them that although healthy, the child has been diagnosed as being German. This is strange because neither of the parents is German or of German descent.

Over the next few years, the child grows and develops normally in every way although after a few years the parents begin to worry that he is late in developing speech.

Numerous tests are carried out but no physiological problem is found. Despite this, year after year goes by and the little boy, although otherwise happy, never speaks a single word.

Eventually on the boy's 16th birthday his mother brings him a bowl of soup while he is sitting silently watching television.

As she leaves the room, she hears a German voice call after her: "Mother, zis soup iz tepid!"

The mother is astonished. "Why, my son!" she cries, "All this time we have been so worried that you have not spoken at all. Why have you waited until this day to say anything to us? To anyone?"

"Well," says the son, "Up until now everyzing haz been zatisfactory."

The Mother-in-law's Cure

A woman comes home one day and finds her mother standing in a bucket of water, holding her arm up so her finger is sticking into the light socket while the woman's husband is standing by the switch. "Hello, dear," says the woman's mother. "George has had this marvellous idea for curing my rheumatism."

The Skydiving Lesson

A man decides to learn to sky dive. He goes up in a plane with his instructor and the instructor says, "You jump out of the plane first. I'll jump out after you and then we'll go down together." The man jumps out, then the instructor jumps out. The man pulls his rip cord and his parachute opens. The instructor pulls his rip cord but his parachute fails to open. The man then sees his instructor plummet past him, frantically trying to get his parachute to open. "Ah!" says the man undoing the straps to his parachute. "So he wants a race, does he?"

The Long Package

A man walks into the Post Office. He tells the assistant, "I need a box 2 inches wide, 2 inches high and 50 yards long." "I beg your pardon," says the assistant. "What on earth do you need that for?" "Well," says the man, "my neighbour's just moved and he's asked me to send him on his garden hose."

Police Investigations

Earlier today a cement lorry collided with the getaway van from a bank robbery. The police say they are looking for five hardened criminals.

A large hole has appeared in the road outside the police station. The police say they are looking into it.

A thief broke into the police station last night and stole the station lavatory seat. The police say they have nothing to go on.

The thief who was caught stealing a calendar was today given twelve months.

Police have found a man lying dead with his face in a bowl of Corn Flakes and milk. They believe it could be the work of a cereal killer.

Police have arrested two men for stealing batteries and fireworks. One was charged and the other was let off.

The Silent Emissions Problem

A man goes to the doctor and says, "I'm having a real problem with silent gas emissions." "How often does this happen?" asks the doctor. "Well," says the man, "in the taxi on the way here I had six silent emissions and the taxi driver didn't notice. In the lift on the way up I had another three silent emissions and the other passengers didn't notice. And since getting here I've already had five silent emissions. What do you think we should do?" "Well," says the doctor, "the first thing we're going to do is check your hearing."

Building A Barbecue

A man walks into a builder's merchants and asks for 25,000 bricks and a two foot square steel mesh. "Why do you need so many bricks?" asks the assistant. "I'm building a barbecue," says the man. "You don't need that many bricks for a barbecue," says the assistant. "Yes I do," says the man, "I live on the top floor of a block of flats."

The Drunk Man At Confession

A drunk staggers into a Catholic church. He finds his way into the confessional and slumps down. After a few moments the priest on the other side of the grille, coughs to try and attract his attention. Still the drunk sits in silence so in the end the priest pounds on the wall. Finally the drunk responds, "Sorry, mate. Can't help you. There's no paper on this side either."

Did You Hear About

Did you hear about the man who invented the door knocker?
He was awarded the No Bell Prize.

Did you hear about the dog that walked into the flea circus?
He stole the show.

Did you hear about the accident involving a lorry full of tortoises colliding with a van full of terrapins?
It was a turtle disaster.

Did you hear about the
man who stuck his face in
the biscuit tin?
He was blinking crackers.

Did you hear about the karate
champion who joined the army?
On his first day, he saluted and
knocked himself unconscious.

Did you hear about the nurse
who swallowed a razor blade?
She gave herself a tonsillectomy,
an appendectomy, a hysterectomy,
and circumcised three of the
doctors on her shift.

Farmer Giles And The Ventriloquist

A ventriloquist is on tour but finds himself in a rural area between shows where he has trouble finding lodgings. Eventually he is directed to Farmer Giles' farm. The old farmer says he will put him up for the night but before he shows him to his room he gives the ventriloquist a tour of the farm.

The ventriloquist decides he will have a bit of fun with the farmer. When Giles shows him his donkey, the ventriloquist says to the animal, "Hello, Mr Donkey. So does the farmer treat you well?" "Oh yes!" he makes the donkey reply. "He gives me carrots and warm straw to lie on."

"That's amazing!" says Farmer Giles, "I've had that animal 20 years and he's never said a word to me!"

Next the farmer shows the ventriloquist his cow. Again the ventriloquist says, "Hello, Mrs Cow. And does the farmer treat you well?" "Oh yes," says the cow, "he milks me every morning and his hands are always lovely and warm."

Again Giles is astounded but before they walk on to the field where he keeps his sheep the farmer stops the ventriloquist and says:

"Actually come to think of it, you better not ask the sheep anything, I know for a fact they tell some terrible lies about me!"

Five Years' Confinement

Three soldiers are caught by the Germans. The Germans tell them they are going to be locked away in solitary confinement for 5 years but they are allowed one last request before they are imprisoned. The first man says, "I would like a five-year supply of beer." So the Germans lock him up with a five-year supply of beer.

The second man says, "I would like a five-year supply of whisky." So the Germans lock him up with a five-year supply of whisky.

And the third man says, "I would like a five-year supply of cigarettes." So the Germans lock him up with a five-year supply of cigarettes.

Five years later the men are finally released. The first man comes out staggering around drunk, the second man comes out and collapses, completely paralytic, and the third man comes out and says, "Has anyone got a light?"

Two Accountants In A Bank Robbery

Two accountants are in a bank. An armed gang of robbers suddenly burst in. They hold up all the bank tellers and they tell everyone else in the bank to line up against the wall. They then go through all the customers' pockets and bags taking all their cash. As the robbers are doing so the first accountant feels the second accountant slip something into his pocket. "What was that?" asks the first accountant. "It's that £50 I owe you," says the second.

Good and Bad News At The Doctor's

A man is suffering terrible pains in his guts. In the end he goes to the doctor's and has some tests done. A few weeks later he is called back to be given the results. "Well," says the doctor, "I've got some good news and some bad news." "OK," says the man, "let's have the good news first." "Well," says the doctor, "they're going to name a disease after you..."

Asking The Bank Manager For A Loan

A man goes into his bank and asks his bank manager, "How do I stand for a £50,000 loan?" "You don't," says the bank manager, "you get down on your knees and you grovel."

Lawyers Are Arseholes!

A man walks into a pub and shouts, "All lawyers are arseholes." "Hey!" says a man in sitting one corner. "I object to that." "Oh yes" says the first man. "So you're some sort of lawyer are you?" "No," says the second man. "I'm an arsehole."

Scottish Taxi Collision

Two taxis collided last night in the middle of Glasgow. According to the police, three people were seriously hurt and the other seventeen escaped with minor injuries.

Three Men In The Desert

Three men are driving across the desert when their car breaks down. There's nothing for it but to walk to the next town which is 50 miles away. Eventually they pass an Arab who notices that the first man is carrying a glass of water.

"Hey!" calls the Arab. "What are you doing carrying that glass of water through the desert."

The first man explains what has happened and that he has a long way to go. For this reason he has taken some water from the car engine to drink during his journey.

The Arab then sees the second man. "Hey!" calls the Arab. "What are you doing carrying that sun visor across the desert?"

The second man explains he has a long way to go and that he has taken the sun visor from the car to shield himself slightly from the hot desert sun.

The Arab then sees the third man who is walking across the desert dragging a car door. "Hey!" calls the Arab. "What are you doing carrying a car door across the desert?"

"Well," says the third man, "I have a long way to go so I pulled the door off the car. I thought if it starts getting a bit too hot I can always roll the window down."

Knock Knock

Knock Knock!
Who's there?
Isobel.
Isobel who?
Isobel necessary on a bicycle?

Knock Knock!
Who's there?
Ivor.
Ivor who?
Ivor good mind not
to tell you.

Knock Knock!
Who's there?
Eva.
Eva who?
Eva you're deaf or your
doorbell isn't working!

Knock Knock!
Who's there?
Shirley!
Shirley who?
Shirley you must know
me by now!

Chatting Up
The Hairdresser's Assistant

A man is sitting at the hairdresser's having a shave. The man takes a shine to the pretty young female assistant who is sweeping up the hair clippings and starts chatting her up. "How about a date tonight?" asks the man. "I can't," says the girl, "I'm married." "No problem," says the man. "Why not just phone your husband and tell him you're going out with a girlfriend this evening?" "Even better," says the girl. "why not ask him yourself? He's the one who's shaving you at the moment."

Two Men Arrested

Two men are arrested for being drunk and disorderly. The policeman asks the first of them, "Where do you live?" "No fixed abode," says the first man. "OK," says the policeman and turns to the second. "So where do you live?" "I live in the flat above him," says the second.

The Amputee's Good News

A man is in hospital after an accident. The doctor comes to his bed and tells him, "I have good news and bad news." "Oh no," says the man. "What's the bad news?" "Your injuries," says the doctor, "turned out to have been very severe and I'm afraid I had no choice but to amputate both your legs." "Oh no," says the man. "So what's the good news?" "Well," says the doctor, "the man in the next bed is interested in buying your slippers."

Elephants

Q: What did Tarzan say to Jane
when he saw the elephants coming
over the hill?

A: *Look, Jane, there are the elephants
coming over the hill!*

Q: What did Tarzan say
to Jane when he saw the
elephants coming over
the hill wearing sunglasses?

A: *Nothing, he didn't recognize
them.*

Q: What is brown, has four
legs, and a trunk?

A: *A mouse coming back
from holiday.*

Q: Why do elephants
paint their toenails red?
A: *So they can hide in
cherry trees.*

Q: How does an elephant get out of a tree?
A: *He sits on a leaf and waits till autumn.*

Q: Why is an elephant big,
grey and wrinkly?
A: *Because if it was small,
white and smooth it would
be an aspirin.*

Q: How do you get down
from an elephant?
A: *You don't, you get
down from a duck.*

The Doctor Hasn't Seen You For A Long Time

A man goes for a doctor's appointment. "I haven't seen you for quite some time," says the doctor. "I know," says the man, "I've not been well."

The Barber's Wooden Balls

A man goes to a barbershop and asks for a shave. The barber starts shaving him and then after a few minutes produces a pair of wooden balls and says, "Here! Just pop these in your mouth so I can get a close shave over your cheeks." The man takes the wooden balls, puts them in between his cheek and gum and the barber shaves over his cheeks. At the end of the shave the man tells the barber, "That was the closest shave I've ever had. There's just one problem. I've accidentally swallowed one of your little wooden balls." "That's OK," says the barber. "Just do what everyone else does. Bring it back tomorrow."

The Drunk Who Falls From A High Building

A drunk falls from the tenth floor of a building.
A crowd gathers around him on the pavement.
A policeman quickly pushes his way through the
crowd, kneels down beside the man and asks, "What
happened here?" "Don't ask me," says the drunk. "I
only just got here myself."

Two Men Doing A Crossword Puzzle

Two men are sitting doing a crossword
puzzle. The first man is about to fill in
an answer. He asks his friend, "How do
you spell paint?" The friend thinks for a
moment and then says, "What colour?"

Going Out With Twins

A man tells his friend that he went on a date
with identical twins last night. "Any luck?"
asks his friend. "Yes and no," says the man.

A Man Walks Into A Chemist

A man walks into a chemist and asks
the assistant for some talcum powder.
"Certainly, sir," says the assistant. "Walk this
way." "If I could walk that way," says the
man, "I wouldn't need the talcum powder."

The Man Under The Cinema Seats

A group of people in a cinema are
trying to watch a film but are being
distracted by an old man crawling
around under the seats. "What are you
doing?" asks a woman. "I'm trying to
find the toffee I dropped," says the
man. "Can't you just leave it?" says the
woman. "Not really," says the man.
"It's got my false teeth stuck in it."

Two Weeks To Live

A doctor tells a patient, "I'm sorry but
you've only got two weeks to live." "OK,"
says the man. "Could I have the last week
in July and the first week in August?"

The Flea Experiment

A scientist gets up at a conference to demonstrate the experiments he has conducted with fleas. He puts a flea on the desk in front of him and shouts, "Jump!" At the sound of the scientist's voice, the flea jumps. The scientist then pulls two of the legs off the flea and shouts, "Jump!" Again the flea jumps. The scientist then pulls two more legs off and again shouts, "Jump!" The flea still manages to jump but then the scientist picks it up and pulls off its remaining two legs. This time when he shouts, "Jump!" the insect doesn't move. "So, gentlemen," says the scientist, "this proves my hypothesis. If you pull the legs off a flea, it will go deaf."

Eggs

A woman goes to the psychiatrist and says, "Doctor, you've got to do something about my husband. He's gone mad and thinks he's a chicken." "Oh dear," says the psychiatrist. "How long has this been going on?" "About a year," says the woman. "A year! Why didn't you bring him in sooner?" "Well," says the woman, "he wasn't hurting anyone and to be honest, we needed the eggs."

The Three Men About To Be Guillotined

During the French Revolution three men are due to be executed on the guillotine.

The first man steps up on the guillotine platform. The executioner says, "You have a choice. You can lie facing down or looking up at the blade."

The first man says he will look up at the blade. They put him in position and drop the blade but half way down it stops.

The executioner tells the man, "The blade has not come down and so according to tradition this means you are free to go."

The first man is released and the second man is brought forward. Again he is given the choice of lying facing down or looking up at the blade and he chooses to look upwards.

Again the blade stops halfway down and again it is decided that according to tradition the second man is free to go.

The third man then steps up. The executioner again gives him the choice of lying facing down or looking up at the blade.

"Well," says the third man, "the other fellers looked up so I'll do the same."

They put him in position and get ready to drop the blade.

"Hang on!" calls the man. " I think I can see what's the matter with your blade!"

The Salesman At The Door

A travelling salesman knocks at a door. The door opens and a little boy looks out. "Hello, little boy," says the salesman, "is your father in?" "No," says the boy, "he went out earlier just before my mother came in." "Oh," says the salesman, "so is your mother in now?" "No," says the boy, "she went out when my brother came in." "Well, is your brother in?" asks the salesman. "No," says the boy, "he went out when I came in." "This is a funny house," says the salesman. "It's not a house," says the boy, "it's our outside toilet."

The Quickest Way To Buckingham Palace

A man walks into a pub in London and asks the barman, "What's the quickest way to Buckingham Palace from here?" "Are you walking or driving?" asks the barman. "Driving," says the man. "Ah yes," says the barman. "That's definitely the quickest way."

The Mole Problem

An ex-military man retires to a big house with a beautiful lawn. One morning he wakes up and sees mole hills all over the grass. He calls for the gardener and tells him to do something about it. Later that day he asks the gardener if he has sorted the mole out yet. "You don't need to worry about that any more, sir," says the gardener. "I caught the little bugger, I took him to the bottom of the garden and I buried him alive!

Changing Light Bulbs

Q: How many thickoes does it take
to change a light-bulb?

A: *Two. One to hold the light-bulb
and one to turn the ladder!*

Q. How many psychoanalysts does
it take to change a light bulb?

A. *Only one – but the light bulb
really has to want to change.*

Q: How many men does it take
to change a light bulb?

A: *Three. One to put in the bulb,
and two to listen to him brag
about the screwing.*

Q: How many folk singers does it take to change a light bulb?

A: *Two – one to change the bulb, and one to write a song about how good the old light bulb was.*

Q: How many policemen does it take to screw in a light bulb?

A: *None. The light bulb turned itself in.*

Q: How many jugglers does it take to change a light bulb?

A: *Only one, but it will take at least three light bulbs.*

Q: How many crime mystery writers does it take to change a light bulb?

A: *Two – one to screw it most of the way in and the other to give it a surprise twist at the end.*

Bird Pooh On The Head

Two men are walking down the road. The first says to the second, "What would you do if a bird pooed on your head?" The second thinks for a moment and says, "I'd probably not go out with her again."

The Air Disaster

The authorities have reported the worst ever air disaster. Early this morning a two seater plane crashed into a graveyard. So far rescue workers have recovered over 4,000 bodies.

The Illegal Turn

A man is driving his son to school when he makes an illegal turn at a set of traffic lights. "Oh no!" says the dad. "I just made an illegal turn." "Don't worry, daddy," says the little boy. "The police car behind us has just done exactly the same thing!"

Two Men Doing A Crossword Puzzle

Two men are sitting doing a crossword puzzle. The first man reads out a clue: "Person who has never had sex. Six letters. Something I something G something something." The second man says, "Is it 'Ginger?'"

The Insufficient Number Of Parachutes

A light aeroplane develops a fault and the pilot has to tell his passengers that they are going to crash and that there aren't enough parachutes on board for all of them.

Besides the pilot, the passengers include a bishop, a scientist and a boy scout.

Before the passengers can take in the dreadful news, the pilot has grabbed one of the parachutes and jumped out of the door.

The scientist, the bishop and the boy scout all look at one another.

"OK," says the scientist, "I'm sorry about this but I am widely regarded as the most intelligent man in Britain. If I don't survive, it will be a terrible loss for science and for mankind."

And with that, the scientist grabs another parachute and jumps out of the plane.

The bishop and the boy scout look at each other.

"Well, my son," says the bishop, "you have all your life ahead of you. The good book tells us to lay down our lives for others and so you must take the final parachute."

"Thank you, your grace," says the boy scout, "but we've still got a parachute each. The most intelligent man in Britain just jumped out of the plane with my rucksack on his back."

Two Irishmen Meet

Two Irishmen meet and one says, "Tell me, have you seen old McQuigley recently?" "Ah well," says the other, "I have and I haven't." "What do you mean by that?" asks the first. "Well," says the other. "I saw a fellow the other day who I thought was McQuigley and he saw a chap that he thought was me. But then when we got up to each other, sure it was neither of us!"

Farmer Giles and his Dog

Farmer Giles is out in the fields trying to count his flock of sheep. In the end he has to get his sheepdog, Shep, to help. Shep runs around the field, counts the sheep and runs back to Farmer Giles. "So," says the farmer, "how many sheep are here?" "One hundred," says the dog. "That's odd," says Farmer Giles. "I only bought 98." "I know," says the dog. "But I just rounded them up for you."

The Scotsman's Trip To London

A Scotsman returns home after a visit to London. A friend asks him how his trip went. "Oh," says the Scotsman, "it was terrible. The Sassenachs are so rude. At three o'clock every morning they were hammering on my bedroom door, shouting and swearing and calling me all the names under the sun." "Och, that's terrible," says his friend. "It certainly is," says the Scotsman. "Sometimes the noise was so bad, I could barely hear myself playing the bagpipes."

Did You Hear About

Did you hear about the man who bought
a plot of land at the North Pole?
*He thought it would be a good place to
grow frozen peas.*

Did you hear about the time
the dresser and the kitchen
unit had a race?
It ended in a drawer.

Did you hear about the hard-living
dyslexic rock star?
He choked to death on his own Vimto.

Did you hear about the human cannonball who lost his job at the circus?
He got fired.

Did you hear about the replacement the circus found for the human cannonball?
He turned not to be of the right calibre.

Did you hear about the dyslexic nurse?
She got into trouble after being asked to prick a patient's boil.

The See Through Underpants

A man walks into a psychiatrist's wearing a pair of see through cellophane underpants. "Well," says the psychiatrist, "I can clearly see you're nuts."

Just Catching The Ferry

A man has to catch the last ferry home each night after work. One night he decides to go for a drink on the way. After a few drinks he realizes he will only just be able to run down to the ferry in time. Not wanting to miss the last boat, he races as quickly as he can but just as he approaches the landing stage he sees the boat eight feet out from the dock. With a final stupendous effort he launches himself across the water and just manages to land on the boat. "Pretty impressive hey!" says the man proudly as he picks himself up off the deck. "Well done," says the captain of the boat. "But why didn't you wait? We were just about to pull in!"

The Businessman's Wives' Testimonials

An airline offers a special deal to businessmen who take their wives on a trip with them. A few weeks later the airline writes directly to the wives to ask them how they enjoyed their trip. Responses then begin pouring in from angry wives all asking, "What trip?"

A Fish Walks Into a Pub

"What can I get you?" asks the barman.
"Just some water," gasps the fish.

My Little Boy Has Swallowed a Teaspoon

A woman runs into the doctor's and says,
"Doctor, my little boy has swallowed a
teaspoon." "Tell him," says the doctor,
"to sit still and not stir."

The Duck Poacher

The gamekeeper catches a man poaching by the side of
the lake. "I saw you," says the gamekeeper, "you were just
plucking that bird and when you heard me approaching
you threw it in the lake." "No," says the man, "I'd
never do that. That duck was my friend." "What do
you mean?" says the gamekeeper. "How do you explain
why you're standing in the middle of a pile of feathers?"
"That's easy!" says the man. "My friend the duck wanted
to go for a swim and I said I'd mind his clothes!"

A Termite Walks Into a Pub

And the termite asks,
"Is the bar tender here?"

Various Professional Peoples' Daughters

She was only an optician's daughter but she didn't half make a spectacle of herself.

She was only a photographer's daughter but she was extremely well developed.

She was only a gravedigger's daughter but she liked to lie under the sod.

She was only a fishmonger's daughter but she'd jump on the slab and say, "Fillet!"

She was only an artist's daughter but she knew where to draw the line.

She was only a doctor's daughter but she really knew how to operate.

She was only a drover's daughter but she could certainly keep her calves together.

She was only a weather forecaster's daughter but she certainly had a warm front.

145

A Private On Sentry Duty

A private is doing sentry duty one night. The phone in the sentry box rings and a pompous voice says, "Are there many cars in the officer's car park tonight?" The sentry checks and then tells his caller, "The only car in the car park is the fat-faced general's Rolls Royce."

"Do you know who you're talking to?" says the voice on the phone. "This IS the general!" "Yes, well," says the private. "Do you know who YOU'RE talking to?" "No I do not," says the general. "Well then bugger off fat face!" says the private, slamming the phone down.

The Busy Barbershop

One morning a barber is at work when a man sticks his head round the shop door and asks, "How long until you can do my hair?"

The barber looks at the row of men waiting and says, "About two hours."

The man nods and leaves. The next day, the man again pokes his head round the door at the busiest time of day. Again he is told there will be a long wait and again he leaves.

This carries on for a week until the barber says to his assistant, "Follow that man, will you? See where he goes after he comes here."

The assistant follows him and returns a few minutes later. "Did you find where he goes each day?" asks the barber. "Yes," says the assistant. "He goes to your house!"

The Non-Stick Frying Pan

A man tells his friend he has just bought a non-stick frying pan. "Is it any good?" asks the friend. "I don't know. I haven't used it yet," says the man. "I can't get the label off it."

How Long Do You Want Your Nails?

A man walks into a hardware shop and says, "I'd like some nails please." "OK," says the assistant. "How long do you want them?" "Well," says the man. "I was hoping I could keep them."

Have You Lived There All Your Life

A man is being interviewed. "Where do you live?" asks the interviewer. "London," says the man. "And have you lived there all your life?" asks the interviewer. "No," says the man. "Not yet."

The Thermos Flask

Two men are sitting on the bus. One notices the other is holding a cylindrical item with a plastic cup on the top. "What's that?" asks the first man. "It's a Thermos Flask," replies the second. "Oh yes," says the first, "what's that for?" "Well," says the second, "it keeps hot things hot and cold things cold." "That's amazing," says the first. "So what have you got in it?" "Two cups of coffee and a choc ice," says the second.

The Devout Man And The Terrible Storm

A terrible storm strikes the town where a devout believer lives. All his neighbours escape but the believer stays in his house because he fervently believes that God will not allow him to perish.

The flood waters rise and he is forced to go up to the first floor. Looking out of the bedroom window he sees a man on a raft go past, calling him to jump aboard.

"No no," says the man. "For I believe God will save me."

The waters continue to rise and he goes up to the attic. Out of the attic window he sees a lifeboat go past. The captain of the lifeboat begs him to get aboard but again he refuses.

Later he is forced to climb onto the roof of the house and is clinging to the chimney when a helicopter flies over head. The pilot of the helicopter beckons him to climb aboard but again the man refuses, placing his trust in God.

The helicopter flies away and the water continues to rise eventually washing the man away.

Standing in line to enter heaven, the man remonstrates with God. "I can't believe this," he says, "I have been a fervent believer all my life and yet you let me die!"

"What are you talking about, you idiot?" says God. "I sent a raft, I sent a lifeboat, I sent a helicopter…"

Question and Answer Session

Q: Which country was once run by napkins?

A: *The Serviette Union.*

Q: What do you get if you drop a grenade on the kitchen floor in France?

A: *Linoleum Blownapart.*

Q: What's dangerous and lives at the bottom of the ocean?

A: *Jack the Kipper.*

Q: What jumps from cake to
   cake and smells of almonds?
A: Tarzipan.

Q: What's green and sings?
A: Elvis Parsley.

Q: How do you turn a duck into
   a soul singer?
A: Put it in the microwave
   until it's Bill Withers.

Q: How do you get the lead
   role in Crossroads?
A: Sit on the radiator until
   you're Googie Withers.

The Businessman Gets Home Late

A businessman misses his train home and doesn't arrive back until the early hours of the morning. When he gets in he finds his wife looking very upset. She tells him, "After I'd switched off the lights and gone to bed, a burglar got into the house and came up the stairs into our bedroom." "Oh no!" says the businessman. "So did he get anything?" "That's the problem," says his wife, "I thought it was you coming in – so yes he did!"

Four Men On A Desert Island

An Englishman, an Irishman, an American and a Scotsman are all washed up on a remote island. Up to now the four of them have not been acquainted. On the island they discover the natives are all friendly and after just a few months the Irishman has set up a farm, the Scotsman has set up a shop and the American is helping them construct a light railway system. Meanwhile the Englishman is still standing alone on the beach waiting to be introduced.

The Scottish Man Goes To The Pub

A Scottish man is watching the TV at home with his wife one evening. Suddenly he gets up, gets ready to go the pub and tells his wife to put her coat on. "Oh!" says his wife surprised. "Are you taking me with you tonight?" "No," says the man. "I'm turning the heating off while I'm out."

The Drunk Driver

A policeman pulls over a car after observing it swerving this way and that across the road. The policeman asks the driver if he has been drinking.

"Yes, I have, occifer," says the driver, "I have just been to the pub where I had a little drinky or three. Then I went to a bar and I had a few more little drinkies, then I went to a club and a had a few more drinkies again and then I got in my car and drove here drinking the bottle of whisky which I still have in the glove compartment."

"Sir," says the policeman, "I would like you to step out of the car and take a breathalyzer test."

"What's'matter," says the driver looking indignant. "Don't you believe me?"

Tips For Married Couples

A married couple decide they need to liven up their sex lives. They therefore go out and purchase a manual which the man eagerly sits down to read.

His wife asks if he has found any helpful advice in the book and he says, "Yes. Apparently it will greatly help our enjoyment if you moan while we are making love."

Later that night the wife decides to give it a go and just as they are reaching their moment of climax she whispers in his ear, "Why do you always leave me to do all the washing up?"

What Do You Put On Your Rhubarb?

A little town boy and a little country boy are playing together in the latter's garden. The little boy from the town looks at a corner of the garden where a pile of horse manure is stacked up. "Ugh!" he says. "What does your dad do with all that manure?" "He puts it on our rhubarb," replies his friend. "You're kidding!" says the little town boy. "We put custard on ours!"

The Stolen Bicycle

A vicar is in church going through the Ten Commandments. As he does so he notices a man in the congregation look suddenly worried but then later breathe a sigh of relief. After the service the vicar asks the man if something had been on his mind. "Yes," says the man, "when you mentioned the commandment 'Thou shalt not steal', I suddenly thought someone had stolen my bicycle. But luckily when you got to the one about 'Thou shalt not commit adultery' I remembered where I'd left it."

The Milk Bath

A milkman is doing his deliveries when a woman comes out of her house and asks if he can deliver 20 gallons of milk. "That's a lot," says the milkman. "I know," says the woman, "but I was just reading that if you bathe in milk it's a wonderful aphrodisiac." "OK," says the milkman, "so you want it pasteurised?" "No," says the woman, "just up to my tits will be fine!"

The Woman With The Glass Eye
From The Flat Upstairs

A man wants to check if it's raining outside. So he sticks his hand out of the window and as he does so a glass eye drops into his palm.

"What's this?" says the man and decides it must have come from the person who lives in the flat above him. He leans out of the window and calls up,

"Hello! Has anyone up there just lost a glass eye?"

"Yes!" shouts a woman's voice. "Could you bring it up to me please."

And so the man goes up the stairs and knocks on the door of the flat above. A woman answers and is very grateful to have her glass eye returned. She invites the man in for a drink. Then she tells him she is about to have dinner and asks if he would like to stay.

Then after the meal she tells him, "I've enjoyed our meal together very much and so I wondered if you might like to stay the night with me."

"My goodness," says the man. "Do you say that to all the men you meet?"

"No," says the woman, "only to the ones who catch my eye."

The Home for The Mentally Infirm

A man is looking round a care home for the mentally infirm. He asks the director, "How do you decide if a person should be committed here?"

"Well," says the director, "we fill a bathtub full of water and offer the person a teaspoon, a tea cup or a bucket and ask him to empty the tub."

"Oh I see," says the man. "A normal person would choose the bucket because it carries more water."

"No," says the director, "a normal person would pull the plug out. So do you want a bed near the window or the door?"

Take These Pills With A Glass Of Water

A man goes to the doctor and says he hasn't been feeling well. The doctor examines him, leaves the room and comes back with three large bottles of differently coloured pills.
The doctor tells the man, "Each morning when you get up you must take one of the green pills with a glass of water. After lunch, take one of the blue pills with a glass of water. And then just before you go to bed, take one of these red pills with a glass of water."
"Gosh!" says the man. "So what exactly is wrong with me?"
"You're not drinking enough water," says the doctor.

Question and Answer Session

Q: What's a polygon?
A: *A dead parrot.*

Q: What's brown and sticky?
A: *A stick.*

Q: What do you call a
   boomerang that doesn't
   come back?
A: *A stick.*

Q: What do you get hanging
from a cherry tree?
A: *Sore arms.*

Q: What's round and
bad tempered?
A: *A vicious circle.*

**Q: What's orange and
sounds like a parrot?**
A: *A carrot.*

Q: What's green and has wheels?
A: *Grass. I lied about the wheels.*

Q: What kind of biscuits does
Bob Marley like?
A: *The ones wi'jam in.*

Aeroplane Engine Problems

In the middle of a flight across the ocean the pilot announces to the passengers:

"Ladies and gentlemen, I'm afraid we have lost the use of one of our engines. There is no need to panic. We still have three engines fully operational. However it does mean that our four-hour flight will instead take six hours."

The passengers settle down again but after another few minutes the pilot makes another announcement.

"I'm afraid we have now lost the use of another engine. Again there is no need to panic. We still have two engines fully functional although it does again mean the flight will take eight rather than six hours."

The passengers settle down again but then hear yet another announcement:

"I'm afraid we have now lost the use of a third engine. There is still no need to panic. The plane is capable of flying on the single engine we have left but it does mean that it will now take us twelve hours to make our journey."

Two passengers are sitting listening.

One leans over to his friend and says, "Let's hope and pray we don't lose that last engine! We could be stuck up here forever."

The Wrong Suit For The Funeral

An old lady is preparing to bury her husband. The funeral directors show her the body laid out. "Oh," she says, "you've got him in a blue suit and I specifically requested to have him buried dressed in brown." "OK," says the funeral director, "we'll get that sorted out for you." As soon as the old lady has gone the funeral director yells, "Hey! Eddie! Swap the heads on number two and number four!"

German Interrogation

During the war, two British POWs get taken for questioning. One is taken into the interrogation room and the other one hears:

"You vill answer ze question!" Slap! Slap! Slap! "You vill answer ze question!" Slap! Slap! Slap! "You vill answer ze question!" Slap! Slap! Slap! "Please stop hitting me and just answer ze question!"

Checking The Indicators

Two men are driving along. The driver becomes worried that one of his rear indicator lights isn't working. He pulls in and asks his friend to go and check the light. The friend goes round to the back of the car while the driver switches the indicator on. "Yes, its working OK," says his friend. "Ah no, it's stopped again. Oh it's started again. No it's stopped again…

Question and Answer Session

Q: What's ET short for?
A: *Because he's got little legs.*

Q: How does a Welshman grate cheese?
A: *Caerphilly.*

Q: What is the fastest cake in the world?
A: *S'gone.*

Q: What does a constipated
mathematician do?
A: *Works it out with a pencil.*

Q: Why do golfers wear two
pairs of trousers?
A: *In case they get a hole in one.*

Q: Why do communists only
drink herbal tea?
A: *Because proper tea is theft.*

Q: What's black and white and red
all over?
A: *A nun falling down the stairs.*

Goodbye Daddy

A father walks past his 5-year-old son's bedroom and hears the little lad saying his prayers.

"God bless mummy," says the boy, "God bless daddy, God bless grandma, goodbye granddad!"

The father thinks this is slightly odd but says nothing about it. The next morning however, the family receives news that the boy's granddad has passed away in the night.

Again that night, the father hears his son praying: "God bless mummy, God bless daddy, goodbye grandma!"

The next morning the family learn that grandma has now passed away.

The dad now thinks his son's clairvoyant abilities are distinctly spooky and a few days later he hears the boy praying, "God bless mummy, goodbye daddy!"

The father is now terrified, he prepares his will, settles his affairs and spends the rest of the day in church preparing for the worst. In the end he returns home only to find his wife looking very upset.

"What's the matter?" he asks.

"A terrible thing happened," says his wife. "Just after you went out this morning I came downstairs and there was the milkman lying dead on the doorstep!"

What Do You Call…

What do you call a man with a spade on his head?
Doug.

What do you call a guy with 50 rabbits stuffed up his backside?
Warren.

What do you call a leper in a hot tub?
Stew.

What do you call a woman
who can balance two pints
of beer on her head?
Beatrix.

What do you
call a camel with
three humps?
Humphrey.

What do you call
a woman who can
balance two pints of
beer on her head while
playing snooker?
Beatrix Potter.

Say You've Got Something Wrong With Your Ear

An old man walks into a crowded doctor's surgery. He goes up to the receptionist and says, "Excuse me. I've got something wrong with my willy." "Get out of here!" says the receptionist crossly. "You must not use language like that in front of the other patients. You should refer to your problem more sensitively. Perhaps say you have something wrong with your ear instead." The next day the old man is back at the doctor's. He walks up to the receptionist and says, "Excuse me. I've got something wrong with my ear." "OK," says the receptionist, "and what seems to be the problem?" "It hurts when I piss out of it," says the old man.

The Hundred and Eleventh Birthday

An old man is celebrating his 111th birthday.
A reporter from the local paper comes to
interview him. "So," says the reporter, "to
what do you attribute your great age?" "Well,"
says the old man, "I think it's mainly to do
with the fact I was born a long time ago."

The International Household

A house is inhabited by a Greek
on the ground floor, an Italian on
the first floor and a German on the
second floor.

One day the house catches fire.
Which of the residents survives?

The German. He was out
practising marching.

The Wife's Inheritance

A man says to his friend, "Did you really only marry your wife because of the money her father left her?" "No of course not," says the friend. "I'd have married her no matter who had given her the money!"

Act Two

A man tells his friend, "I went to the theatre with my wife last night but we couldn't wait for the second half." "What happened?" asks the friend. "Well," says the man, "it said in the programme, 'Act Two: Two Weeks Later'."

You Can't Eat Your Own Food In Here

Two men are sitting in a café eating their packed lunches. The manager comes over and says, "I'm sorry, gents, but you're not allowed to eat your own food in here." So they swap.

The Injured Hand

A man is having his broken hand bandaged by the doctor. "Tell me, doctor," says the man. "Will I be able to play the piano when my hand gets better?" "Oh yes," says the doctor. "I expect so." "Oh that's good!" says the man. "I couldn't before!"

Question and Answer Session

Q: What's black and runny?
A: *Linford Christie.*

Q: What's black, has long ears and smokes?
A: *A rabbit chewing an electric cable.*

Q: What's pink and wrinkly and hangs out your underpants?
A: *Your mum.*

Q: What's red and invisible?
A: *No tomatoes.*

Q: What's red and smells like blue paint?
A: **Red paint.**

Q: What's green and misty?
A: *Kermit the Fog.*

Q: What's black and white and red all over?
A: *A homicidal panda.*

The Three Smiling Corpses

Three bodies are lying in the chapel of rest. The funeral director is showing them to his new assistant. The assistant notices that all three bodies have enormous great smiles across their faces and asks what happened to them.

"Ah well this first one," says the funeral director, "had just got 6 numbers on the lottery. The surprise was so great he immediately had a heart attack and that's why he died with a big smile on his face. The second man here died on his honeymoon with his beautiful new bride. He had a stroke while in a state of ecstasy with her and that's why he died with a big smile on his face."

"OK," says the assistant. "So what happened to the third man? Had something nice just happened to him as well?"

"No," says the funeral director. "He got struck by lightning."

"So why is he smiling?" asks the assistant.

"He thought someone was taking his photo," says the funeral director.

The Obese Woman At The Doctor's

An obese woman goes to the doctor for a check up. The obese woman is rather ashamed of her appearance and says, "I'm sorry, doctor. I've rather let myself ago." "Not at all," says the doctor holding up a tongue depressor. "Now just open your mouth and say 'Moooo'!"

Avoiding The Dog Mess

Two tramps are walking down the street when one suddenly grabs the other. "Careful!" he says. "You nearly trod in that dog mess." "Is it really dog mess?" says his friend. "We'd better check," says the first. So they bend down, they peer at the mess, one sniffs it, the other sticks his finger in it, they each scoop some up and finally they both taste it. "Ugh!" they both cry. "That's disgusting!" "Yes," says one, "that's definitely dog mess." "Yes," says his friend, "thank goodness we didn't step in it!"

Farmer Giles' Feed Order

Farmer Giles phones up his animal feed supplier, wanting to make an order. The supplier says, "I'm sorry, Farmer Giles. I notice in our books that you haven't paid us yet for your last lot of feed or for the one before that. I'm afraid in the circumstances we can't send you out the new order until the last two have been paid for." "You bastard!" says Farmer Giles. "How do you expect me to wait that long?"

A Call From The Husband

A woman is at home in bed with her husband's best friend when the phone rings. The woman answers, has a brief conversation and hangs up. "Who was that?" asks the man. "That was my husband," says the woman. "Oh no!" says the man. "Calm down and stop looking so worried!" says the woman. "He says he's out playing cards with you!"

175

Waiter!

"Waiter, this plate is wet."
"No, it's not wet, sir.
That's the soup."

"Waiter, why is this beetle
floating in my soup?"
"Well, they're not very good
swimmers, you see."

"Waiter, there's a fly in my soup!"
"Sorry about that, sir. The dog
must have missed it."

"Waiter, there's a fly in my soup!"
"I know. I think it's the rotting meat
that attracts them."

"Waiter, there's a fly in my soup!"
"Sorry, sir. Did you want it
served separately?"

"Waiter, this food isn't fit
for a pig!"
"I'm sorry about that, sir. I
shall take it away and bring
you some that is."

"Waiter, why is your
thumb on my steak?"
"I don't want it to fall
on the floor again."

"How did you find your steak, sir?"
"I just moved a potato and there it was."

The Siamese Twins On Holiday

Two Siamese twins arrive on holiday in England. They book into a hotel and the manager says, "Weren't you here last year?"

"Yes," says one of the twins. "We come here every year from our home in the south of France."

"You come here from the south of France?" says the manager looking puzzled. "Do you like it here?"

"No," says the other twin. "We hate it. The weather's lousy, the food's awful and everyone's so bloody rude."

"Oh," says the manager, "so why do you keep coming?"

"Well," says the twin on the left. "It's the only chance my brother here gets to drive."

Small Man On A Plane

A small man is on a plane sitting next to the window when a mean looking giant of a man comes and sits in the seat next to him. A few minutes into the flight, the giant is fast asleep but the small man has begun to feel airsick. The small man is afraid to wake his neighbour up to get past to the toilet and is wondering what to do when suddenly he can't hold it any more and he throws up all over his neighbour's chest.

A moment later, the giant wakes up and looks at the sick all down his front. He turns to the small man next to him, who says, "Are you feeling a little bit better now then?"

Skoda Jokes

Q: What do you call a
Skoda with a sun roof?
A: *A skip.*

Q: What do you
call a Skoda with
a seatbelt?
A: *A rucksack.*

Q: What do you call a Skoda
with an aerial?
A: *A bumper car.*

Q: How do you overtake
   a Skoda?
A: *Walk quicker.*

Q: What do a Skoda and a
   baby have in common?
A: *Neither of them goes
   anywhere without a rattle.*

Q: **Why did the Skoda cross the road?**
A: *The steering failed.*

Q: What's the difference between a
   Skoda and a sheep?
A: *It's less embarrassing being
   caught getting out of the back of
   a sheep.*

Knock Knock

Knock Knock!
Who's there?
Irish stew.
Irish stew who?
Irish stew in the name of the law.

Knock Knock!
Who's there?
Oscar.
Oscar who?
Oscar silly question,
get a silly answer!

Knock Knock!
Who's there?
Yvonne.
Yvonne who?
Yvonne to be alone!

Knock Knock!
Who's there?
Lettuce.
Lettuce who?
Lettuce in and we'll
tell you.

Knock, knock!
Who's there?
Idunnop.
Idunnop who?
Have you? Yes, I thought I
could smell something.

Pet Names

I call my dog blacksmith.
Every time anyone calls, he
makes a bolt for the door.

I call my dog handyman.
He keeps doing odd jobs
all over the house.

I call my horse Flattery.
He gets me nowhere.

I call my cat Grandmaster Flash.
He never stops scratching.

I call my cat the
Cerebrovascular Doctor.
He won't let anyone have
a stroke.

I call my cat The Truth.
Very few people are able
to handle it.

I call my dog Bungee Rope.
He keeps snapping.

I call my dog Woodbine.
I take him out for a drag
every evening.

I call my dog Excellent
Homework.
He's covered in ticks.

I call my dog Pharoah.
He leaves pyramids
everywhere he goes.

I call my dog the Horticultural
Entrepreneur. He's always
doing his business in people's
gardens.

I call my pet
amphibian Tiny.
He's my newt.

Crossing The Road

Q: Why did the hedgehog cross the road?
A: *He wanted to visit his flat mate.*

Q: Why did the duck cross the road?
A: *He'd been employed by the chicken's wife to keep her husband under covert surveillance and find out where he was going each day.*

Q: Why did the one-handed man cross the road?
A: *To get to the second hand shop.*

Q: Why did the tomato cross the road?
A: *He wanted to ketchup his friends.*

Q: Why did the chewing gum cross the road?
A: *It was stuck to the chicken's foot.*

Q: Why did the egg cross the road?
A: *Because the chicken had come first.*

Q: Why did the Beatles cross the road?
A: They needed a picture for one of their album covers.

189

The Pope in The Driving Seat

The Pope arrives in the country on an official papal visit. He is picked up by a chauffeur in a beautiful limousine. The Pope cannot resist asking, "Would it be OK if I have a go driving the car for a while?"

"OK," says the chauffeur and he and the Pope swap places.

The Pope sets off and begins to really enjoy driving the car. He accelerates up to 80 mph and is spotted by two policemen. The policemen pursue him and pull him over. One of the policemen goes over to the car to have a word with the driver.

A moment later he comes back to ask his colleague's advice.

"We've got a situation here," says the policeman. "We've just pulled over a major league VIP."

"Who is it?" asks his colleague. "Did you recognize him?"

"No, I didn't," says the policeman. "But whoever he is, he's got the Pope for his chauffeur."

Cotton Wool Balls

A man walks up to the counter in a chemist's shop and says, "Excuse me. Have you got cotton wool balls?" "What do you think I am?" says the assistant. "A teddy bear?"

Likelihood of Plane Crashes

A man asks the stewardess on a plane, "Do these planes crash often?" "No!" says the stewardess. "Only once."

The Wife Who Is Always Asking For Money

A man tells his friend, "My wife is terrible. She is always asking me for money. Every morning, noon and night she never stops." "Oh my goodness," says his friend. "So what does she spend it all on?" "I don't know," says the man. "I never give her any."

Fire and Theft Policy

A man phones up an insurance company and asks for a quote for a fire and theft policy on his car. "It's £5," says the insurance clerk. "Five pounds!" says the man. "That sounds a bit cheap!" "Not really," says the insurance clerk. "Who's going to steal a burning car?"

The Vicar and the Hotel Porn Channel

A vicar is booking into a hotel. As he does so, he says to the receptionist, "I hope the porn channel in my room is disabled?" "No!" says the receptionist. "It's just normal porn, you sick bastard!"

Knock Knock

Knock Knock!
Who's there?
Mandy!
Mandy who?
Mandy lifeboats,
the ship is
sinking!

Knock Knock!
Who's there?
Sam and Janet.
Sam and Janet who?
Sam and Janet
evening, you may see a
stranger...

Knock, Knock!
Who's there?
Madam.
Madam who?
Madam finger is
stuck in the door!

Knock Knock!
Who's there?
Cowsgo! Cowsgo who?
No, cows don't go who,
cows go moo!

Knock, knock!
Who's there?
Woo.
Woo, who?
OK, no need to get so excited.
It's just a joke.

Have You Heard The Joke About...

Have you heard the joke
about the cheese biscuit?
It's a cracker.

Have you heard the
joke about the skunk?
It stinks.

Have you heard the joke
about the fence?
I just can't get over it.

Have you heard the joke
about the vacuum cleaner?
It sucks.

**Have you heard the joke about
the dog with the sore foot?**
It's a bit lame.

**Have you heard the joke about
the ledge just under the window?**
It's a bit sill-ie.

Have you heard the joke about
the condom that promises
enhanced sensual pleasure?
It's a real ribbed tickler.

Have you heard the joke about the
Old English sheepdog that voted
Conservative in the last election?
It's a shaggy dog's Tory.

Two Snakes

One snake says to another,
"Are we poisonous?" "Yes,"
says the other snake. "Oh
dear!" says the first. "I just
bit my tongue!"

Helicopter
Flavour Crisps

A man walks into a pub and
asks the barman if they have
any helicopter flavour crisps.
"No," says the barman.
"We only have plain."

The Insomniac Boxer

A boxer goes to the doctor's suffering from terrible insomnia. "Have you tried counting sheep?" suggests the doctor. "No, that doesn't help at all," says the boxer. Every time I reach nine, I get up."

Found Not Guilty

A man is up in court for embezzlement and spends his entire trial desperately protesting his innocence. Eventually the jury find him not guilty and he turns with a look of joy and relief to the judge.

"Thank you so much, your honour!" he says "So does this mean I can keep the money?"

I Think I'm a Goat

A man goes into the doctor's and says, "I think I'm a goat." "How long have you felt like this?" asks the doctor. "Ever since I was a kid," says the man.

An Englishman, an Irishman and A Frenchman

An Irishman, an Englishman and a Frenchman are walking along the beach one day and find a lantern. They give it a rub and out pops a genie. "Right," says the genie. "You can have one wish each."

"OK," says the Irishman, "I am a fisherman, my father was a fisherman and my son will be a fisherman too. So I wish all the world's oceans will be full of fish for all eternity." The genie claps his hands and POOF the Irishman's wish is granted.

Next the Frenchman steps up and says, "I am a fiercely proud citizen of France, my father was a proud Frenchman and my son is a proud Frenchman too. So I want a wall around France to stop anyone else getting in and ruining the place!" Again the genie claps his hands and POOF the Frenchman's wish is granted.

Finally the Englishman steps up and asks for a bit more information about the Frenchman's wall. "Well," says the genie. "It's 150 feet high, 50 feet thick and it protects France so that nothing can get in or out."

"Excellent," says the Englishman, "my wish then is for it be filled to the top with water!"

Question and Answer Session

Q: What's the difference between a hedgehog and a 4x4?

A: *The hedgehog has the pricks on the outside.*

Q: **What's the difference between a trampoline and a lawyer?**

A: ***You take your shoes off before you jump on a trampoline.***

Q: What's the difference between a dead rabbit on the road and a dead lawyer on the road?

A: *The rabbit has skid marks in front of it.*

Q: What's the difference
   between a cross eyed
   hunter and a constipated owl?
A: *One shoots but cannot hit...*

Q: What's the difference
    between a nun in church
    and a nun in the bath?
A: *One has hope in her soul...*

Q: What's the difference between a
   bogey and some spinach?
A: *You can't get your children to eat
    spinach.*

Jewellery Shopping

A man and a woman are walking down the street and stop in front of a jewellery store. "Ooh!" says the woman. "Look at that beautiful necklace? Will you get it for me?" "No problem, darling," says the man and whips out a brick and chucks it through the shop window before grabbing the necklace. Later on they stop in front of another jewellery shop and the woman says, "Oooh! Look at that beautiful bracelet. Will you get it for me?" "No problem, darling," says the man and smashes the window with another brick so he can grab the bracelet. A bit later on they stop in front of another jewellery store. "Ooooh!" says the woman. "Look at that beautiful diamond ring. Will you get it for me?" "Hoi!" says the man. "What do you think I am? Made of bricks?"

Wife Wanted

A man puts an advert in the paper that reads: "Wife wanted."
The next day he is inundated with hundreds of replies, every one of which says the same thing: "You can have mine!"

The Escaped Lion

A man sees a group of people running terrified down the road towards him. The man asks one of them, "What are you all running for?" "A lion has escaped from the zoo!" says a woman in the crowd. "Oh no!" says the man. "Which way is it heading?" "Well, I'll give you a clue," says the woman. "We're not chasing it!"

Jokes About Idiots

Insert the group or person of your choice in place of the word idiot

Did you hear about the idiot
who opened a paper shop?
It blew away.

Did you hear about the idiot
who was stranded on a desert
island?
*One day a lifeboat washed up
on the shore so he broke it up to
make a raft.*

Did you hear about the idiot
park keeper whose boss told him
to go and sweep up the leaves?
He fell out of a tree.

Did you hear about the
idiot Sea Scout?
*He went camping and his
tent sank.*

Did you hear about the
idiot firing squad?
They stood in a circle.

Did you hear about
the idiot's parachute?
It opens on impact.

Question and Answer Session

Q: What's the difference between
   roast beef and pea soup?
A: *Anyone can roast beef.*

Q: What's the difference between a
   violin and a viola?
A: *The viola burns for slightly longer.*

Q: What's the difference
   between a snowman
   and a snowwoman?
A: *Snow balls.*

Q: What's the difference between a cross country run and Gordon Ramsey?

A: *One is a pant in the country...*

Q: What's the difference between an accordion and an onion?

A: *No one cries when you chop up an accordion.*

Q; What's the difference between a Rottweiler humping your leg and a poodle humping your leg?

A: *You let the Rottweiler finish.*

A Man Walks Into a Scottish Bakery

A man walks up to the counter in a bakery in Scotland. "Is that a macaroon in the window," he asks, "or a meringue?" "No, you're quite right," says the assistant. "It's a macaroon."

A Beautiful Woman And Her Doctor

A beautiful woman asks her doctor, "Doctor, please will you give me a kiss." "Goodness me, no!" says the doctor. "That would be completely against my code of ethics." "Oh please," begs the woman. "Just one kiss!" "Certainly not," says the doctor. "Strictly speaking we shouldn't even be having sex."

Two Small Children Peering Into A Nudist Camp

Two small children find a hole in the fence by a nudist camp. One peers in through the hole. The other asks, "Are they men or ladies in there?" "I can't tell," says the first. "None of them have got any clothes on."

The Marriage of Two TV Aerials

Two TV aerials meet, fall in love and get married. Everyone agreed afterwards that the ceremony had been awful, but the reception was excellent.

A Favour From Frank Sinatra

A man takes his girlfriend to Las Vegas on a special holiday. While he's there he spots Frank Sinatra in the lobby of a hotel. The man is a big Sinatra fan and so he sidles up to his hero and says: "Mr Sinatra, it's absolutely fantastic to meet you. I have all your records and have seen all your films. I wonder if I could ask a favour of you."

"OK," says Frank. "What is it?"

"I'm here with my girlfriend," says the man, "it would impress her so much if you came over to us in the bar in a few minutes and said hello to me as though we were old pals."

"Ah what the hell!" says Sinatra. "OK I'll do it!"

A few minutes later the man is sitting at the bar with his girlfriend. Frank walks over to them, taps the man on the shoulder and says, "Hey! Fancy meeting you here! How you doing?"

The man turns and says, "Oi! Piss off, Frank! Can't you see I'm busy?!"

Shakespeare's Skull

A man is looking round a museum in Stratford on Avon. In one of the cases he notices a human skull and asks the guide what it is. "That's our most precious exhibit, sir," says the guide. "That is the actual skull of William Shakespeare." "It looks a bit small," says the man. "Well, yes," says the guide looking slightly embarrassed, "that's because it was Shakespeare's skull when he was a boy."

Emergency Services Call Out

A man tells his friend, "I don't think my wife likes me very much. When I had a heart attack she wrote for an ambulance."

The Jewish Grandmother At The Beach

An elderly Jewish lady takes her grandchild to the beach. Suddenly a huge wave crashes onto the beach and the little boy is pulled out to sea. "Oi vay!" says the grandmother. "Please God, save my only grandson! He is my life. He is the future of our family! With all my years of faith, please return him to us safely!" And at that exact moment a huge wave rolls back onto the beach carrying the little lad with it and depositing him slightly damp but otherwise none the worse for wear. The grandmother looks at the boy then looks up at the sky and calls, "He had a hat!"

How To Remember Where All The Fish Are

Two men rent a boat and go out on a lake fishing. They catch a load of fish and one says, "This is a great spot. We'll have to come back here again tomorrow." "But," says the other, "how are we going to remember exactly where we found all the fish?" "That's easy," says the first producing a marker pen, "we'll just draw an X right here on the bottom of the boat." "You idiot!" says his friend. "That's never going to work! How do you know we'll get to rent the same boat tomorrow?"

Jokes About Idiots

Insert the group or person of your choice in place of the word idiot

Did you hear about the idiot traffic warden?
He booked a steamroller for having bald tyres.

Did you hear about the idiot who got sacked from his job in the banana factory?
He kept throwing out all the bent ones.

Did you hear about the idiot lorry driver?
He drove over a cliff because he wanted to test his air brakes.

Did you hear about the
idiot letter bomber?
*He put his own name and
address on the back of parcel
under the heading: "In case
of non-delivery…"*

Did you hear about the idiots'
space expedition?
*They didn't manage to get their
rocket to lift off because they
couldn't find a milk bottle big
enough.*

**Did you hear about the idiots who
tried to climb Mount Everest?**
They ran out of scaffolding.

The Taxi Driver's Riddle

A man goes on a business trip to Liverpool during the course of which he has to make a long journey by taxi. During the journey, the driver decides to break the monotony and says to the man, "Do you like riddles?"

"Oh yes," says the man, "I think so."

"OK," says the taxi driver. "Try this one: 'Brothers and sisters have I none, but this man's father is my father's son.' Who is it?"

The man tries to work out the puzzle but in the end says, "No. It's no good. I can't do it? Who is it?"

"It's me!" says the taxi driver. "Think about it!"

216

'Oh yes!" says the man. "Very good!"

The rest of the journey passes in silence.
A few days later the man is back home
again where he decides to try the riddle
out on a friend.

'Do you like riddles?" he asks his friend.

'Oh yes!" says the friend.

'Right!" says the man. "Try this one:
'Brothers and sisters have I none, but this
man's father is my father's son.'
Who is it?"

The friend thinks and thinks and in the
end says: "No, it's no good. I can't get it."

'Ha! It's easy!" says the man. "It's a taxi
driver from Liverpool!"

Question and Answer Session

Q: What's the difference between a
hungry man and a glutton?

A: *One longs to eat, one eats too long.*

Q: **What's the difference
between a photocopier and
bubonic plague?**

A: *One makes facsimiles, the
other makes sick families.*

Q: What's the difference
between an Irish wedding
and an Irish funeral?

A: *One less drunk.*

Q: What's the difference
    between a heroic
    soldier and an evil baker?
A: *The soldier darts into*
    the foe…

Q: What's the difference between a
bad golfer and a bad skydiver?
A: *One goes "Whack!… Damn!" the*
other goes "Damn!… Whack!"

Q: What's the difference
    between a rock guitarist and
    a jazz guitarist?
A: *A rock guitarist plays three*
    chords in front of a thousand
    fans…

The Huge Man And The Half Loaf

A huge man with a shaved head and enormous tattooed arms walks into a bakery. The boy behind the counter asks, "What can I get you, sir?" The man indicates a loaf of bread on the shelf and says, "I want that loaf but I only want half of it." "I'm sorry, sir," says the boy, "but we don't sell half loaves." "I want half of that loaf!" demands the gigantic man.

The boy goes in to the back of the shop to ask his boss what to do. "This enormous ugly great lunkhead just walked in," he says, "and asked to buy half a loaf." Just at that moment the boy becomes aware that the man has followed him and is standing in the doorway.

"And then this gentleman," stammers the boy, "came in and asked if he could buy the other half!"

220

The Old Lady's Complaint

A policeman is called round to an old lady's house. "It's the man next door," she tells him. "It's absolutely disgusting. I can see right into his house from my bedroom and he wanders round all day with the curtains wide open naked as the day he was born."

The policeman is very concerned and looks out of the window to check on this exhibitionist next door. "Just a minute!" says the policeman. "I don't seem to be able to see into your neighbour's house at all from here."

"Oh you can," says the old lady, "if you climb on top of the wardrobe!"

Idiot Inventions

The chocolate teapot

The inflatable dartboard

The solar powered torch

The fireproof match

The waterproof sponge

The silent alarm clock

The black highlighter pe

Smooth sandpaper

The helicopter ejector seat

The glass hammer

Non-stick sellotape

The Braille speedometer

The waterproof teabag

Old Communist Jokes From The Other Side Of The Iron Curtain

A comrade has saved his money to buy a car. He goes to the dealership to place his order.

"Your car will arrive in seven years," says the salesman.

"Will that be in the morning?" asks the comrade.

"What difference does it make?" says the salesman.

"I have to know," says the comrade. "I've got the plumber coming in the afternoon."

A man dies and is offered a choice of capitalist hell and communist hell. He goes to the door for capitalist hell and asks, "What's it like inside?" "It's terrible," says the doorkeeper. "In capitalist hell, we'll flay you alive, we'll boil you in oil and we'll cut you into pieces with sharp knives."

The man goes to the door for communist hell and notices a long queue of people waiting to get in. "What's it like inside?" he asks. "It's terrible," says the doorkeeper. "In communist hell, we'll flay you alive, we'll boil you in oil and we'll cut you into pieces with sharp knives." "But that's exactly the same as capitalist hell!" says the man. "So why have you got such a big queue?"

"Well," says the doorkeeper. "Sometimes we're out of oil, sometimes we don't have knives, sometimes no hot water…"

An Englishman, a Frenchman and a Soviet are in an art gallery looking at a painting of Adam and Eve.

"Look at their calm and reserve," says the Englishman. "They must be English."

"Non," says the Frenchman. "They are so beautiful, they must be French."

"Nyet," says the Soviet. "They have no clothes, they have no shelter, they only have one apple between them and yet they're being told they are in paradise. They must be Soviets!"

Q: How can you use a banana as a compass?

A: *Place it on top of the Berlin Wall. The side with a bite taken out of it is east.*

226

Alexander the Great, Caesar and Napoleon all meet at a communist parade in Red Square.

"Damn!" says Alexander watching the parade. "If I'd had those tanks, I would have been invincible!"

"Damn!" says Caesar. ""If I'd had those missiles, I would have conquered the entire world!"

"Damn!" says Napoleon. "If I'd had Pravda, no-one would have heard about Waterloo yet!"

The Multi-Coloured Car

Two drivers are talking. One of the drivers notices that the other has one side of his car painted green and the other side painted red. "Well, you see that's for when I get into an accident," explains the other driver. "The police always believe my version of events because the witnesses always contradict each other."

The Empty Glass

A man is sitting at a table in a pub. His friend walks in and notices him. "I see your glass is empty," says the friend. "Shall I get you another?" "Don't be stupid," says the man, "why would I want two empty glasses?"

Free Drinks

An Englishman, an Irishman and a Scotsman are sitting in a pub reminiscing about their home towns. "In my local in Glasgae," says the Scotsman, "fer every four pints of heavy I order, they give me one fer free." "Well," says the Irishman, "in my local in Dublin, for every two pints of Guinness I order, they give me two more free." "That's nothing," says the Englishman. "I know this pub in London where you get given your first pint for free, your second pint for free and your third pint for free. And then they take you upstairs and give you sex for free." "Rubbish!" say the other two. "Has that really ever happened to you?" "OK. Not to me," says the Englishman. "But it happens to my sister quite regularly."

Husband Going To The Doctor's

A man bumps into a friend as he
hurries down the street. "I'm going to
the doctor's," says the man.
"I don't like the look of my wife."
"I'll come with you," says the friend.
"I can't stand the sight of mine."

Soldiers Who Enjoy Music

A company are on parade when
the sergeant major says, "Right,
are any of you men fond of
music?" Three or four of the men
respond and the sergeant major
tells them, "Right, excellent. Fall
out and report for shifting the
canteen piano."

The Dog's Business On The Pub Floor

A man walks into a pub and as he walks to the bar he slips over and falls on his backside. He gets up, looks at what he's just trodden in and sees that the landlord's dog has done its business in the middle of the floor. The man, feeling rather embarrassed, orders a drink. A moment later the pub door is thrown open and a huge great biker strides in. The biker also slips on the dog's business and lands on his backside. The biker picks himself up and looks at what he's just trodden in. The biker then notices the man at the bar laughing at him. "I just did that!" says the man cheerfully. So the biker picks him up and rubs his nose in it.

Question and Answer Session

Q: What's the difference between a
businessman and a warm dog?

A: *The businessman wears a suit, the
dog just pants.*

Q: What's the difference between a
chiropodist and a drummer?

A: *A chiropodist bucks up your feet.*

Q: What's the difference
between a golf ball and
a G-spot?

A: *A man will spend 20
or 30 minutes looking
for a golf ball.*

Q: What's the difference between a lawn mower and a bagpipe?
A: *You can tune a lawn mower.*

Q: What's the difference between a musician and a mutual fund?
A: *Eventually the mutual fund will mature and start earning money.*

Q: What's the difference between a Scotsman and a coconut?
A: *You can get a drink out of a coconut.*

The Cut Price Dentist

A man walks into a dentist's surgery and asks how much it costs to remove a tooth.

"One hundred pounds," says the dentist.

"Oh dear, that's a lot," says the man. "Is there any way you can get the price down a bit?"

"Well," says the dentist, "I could not use any anaesthetic. That will knock it down to £50."

"OK," says the man. "Anything else you can do to make it a bit cheaper?"

"I could just use a pair of pliers," says the dentist. "That would get it down to £15."

"That's still slightly more than I wanted to pay," says the man.

"OK," says the dentist, "we'll do it without anaesthetic, using the pliers and I'll get one of my students on work experience to do it. The price will then be £5."

"Excellent," says the man.

"OK," says the dentist making a note of the appointment. "So what is your name?"

"Oh it's not for me," says the man. "It's for my wife."

Jokes About Idiots

Insert the group or person of your choice in place of the word idiot

Did you hear about the idiot grandmother who went on the pill. *She said she didn't want to have any more grandchildren?*

Did you hear about the idiot athlete who won a gold medal? *He was so pleased, he had it bronzed.*

Did you hear about the idiot who heard that most car accidents happened within two miles of home? *He moved.*

Did you hear about
the idiot pirate?
*He had a patch over
each eye.*

Did you hear about the idiot
who tried to blow up a car?
*He burnt his mouth on the
exhaust pipe.*

Did you hear about the idiot
who reversed his car into a car
boot sale?
He ended up selling his engine.

Question and Answer Session

Q: What do you get if you cross a snowman with a vampire?

A: *Frostbite.*

Q: What do you get if you cross a birthday cake with a tin of baked beans?

A: *A cake that blows out its own candles.*

Q: What do you get if you cross a thief with an orchestra?

A: *Robbery with violins.*

Q: What do you get if you cross
a Labrador with a tortoise?

A: *An animal that comes back
from the newsagent's with last
week's newspaper.*

Q: What do you get if you
cross a giraffe and a dog?

A: *An animal that likes to
chase low flying aeroplanes.*

Q: What do you get if
you cross a hen with a
bedside clock?

A: *An alarm cluck.*

Q: What do you get if
you cross a chicken
with a cement mixer?

A: *A brick-layer.*

The Chalk Circle

An idiot driver gets into an altercation with an enormous hairy biker. The biker gets past him and blocks the road. "Right, get out of your car!" demands the biker.

The man gets out. The biker produces a piece of chalk and draws a circle on the ground. "Right, you step inside that circle," the biker tells him, "and don't step out of it until I tell you."

The man steps inside the circle and watches as the biker scratches his car's paintwork. The biker looks back at the man and sees that he is laughing. The biker then smashes the headlights but the man laughs even harder. Finally the biker produces a hammer and smashes all the car's windows. Now the man is laughing helplessly.

"What's so funny!?" screams the biker. "I've just completely smashed up your car!"

"I know," sniggers the man. "But every time you turned your back I stepped out of the circle!"

A Man Shows A Sheep To His Wife

A woman is sitting in bed when her husband walks into the bedroom with a sheep under his arm. "This," he says, "is the pig I make love to when you say you have a headache." "I think," says his wife, "you'll find that that is a sheep." "I was taking to the sheep!" says the man.

Jokes About Idiots

Insert the group or person of your
choice in place of the word idiot

Did you hear about the idiot
who crashed his helicopter?
He said he turned the fan off
because it was too noisy.

Did you hear about the idiot
dog who sat chewing a bone
in front of the fire?
When he got up, he walked
away on three legs.

Did you hear about the
idiot kamikaze pilot?
He had flown eight
successful missions.

Did you hear about the idiot
who took up Morris dancing?
He kept falling off the bonnet.

Did you hear about the idiot
parachutist?
He got lost on the way down.

Did you hear about the
idiot who was buried at sea?
*Four of his friends drowned
digging the hole.*

The Gangrenous Pilot

During the war, a British pilot is shot down over Germany and sustains terrible injuries. He regains consciousness and finds himself in hospital with a German doctor at his bedside. The doctor explains, "Your injuries are severe. Your right leg was crushed so badly, we had to amputate it. I realize how terrible this must seem but please ask if I can do anything to comfort you."

"There is something, doctor," says the pilot. "Give my amputated leg to the Luftwaffe and ask them to drop it over England on their next mission. I would feel better if my leg wound up back home."

And so the doctor gives the amputated leg to an officer of the Luftwaffe to drop over England. Two days later however, there is more bad news. The pilot's left leg also has to be amputated. Again he asks for it to be dropped over England. Another week later and there is yet more bad news. Both of his arms now have to be amputated. Again he requests that they are dropped over England.

This time, however, the Luftwaffe officer insists on speaking with the pilot. "You are the pilot who wanted his right leg dropped over England." asks the officer.

"Yes," says the pilot.

"And then you wanted your left leg dropped over England. And now both your arms also?" says the officer.

"That is correct," says the pilot.

"Hmm," says the officer looking suspicious. "Tell me something … you're not trying to escape, are you?"

Question and Answer Session

Q: What do you get if you cross an octopus with a cow?

A: *An animal that is capable of milking itself.*

Q: What do you get if you cross a sheepdog with a sheep?

A: *An animal that can round itself up.*

Q: What do you get if you cross a pig with a nudist?

A: *Streaky bacon.*

Q: What do you get if you cross a sheep with a kangaroo?

A: *A woolly jumper.*

Q: What do you get if you
cross a cockerel with a dog?
A: *A cocker-poodle-doo.*

Q: What do you get if you cross an
elephant with a kangaroo?
A: *Enormous great holes all over
Australia.*

Q: What do you get if you cross
Lassie with a pit bull?
A: *A dog that attacks you and
then runs to fetch help.*

Q: What do you get if you cross
a cowboy with an octopus?
A: *Billy the squid.*

The Penguins In The Car

A man is driving down the road when he is pulled over by a policeman. When the policeman comes to take his details, he notices three penguins sitting side by side on the back seat.
The policeman asks the driver what he is doing with three live penguins in his car.

"Oh, I found them standing by the road," explains the driver, "and now I don't know what to do with them."

"Well, sir," says the policeman, "my advice would be to take them to the zoo."

The next day, the policeman stops the man again and is astonished to see the penguins still sitting on the back seat, now wearing sunglasses.

"I thought I told you to take these penguins to the zoo," says the policeman.

"I did," says the man, "and they enjoyed it so much that today I'm taking them to the seaside!"

Memory For Faces

A man books into
a seedy hotel. The
receptionist asks him,
"Do you have a good
memory for faces?"
"Yes," says the man.
"Why do you ask?"
"There's no mirror
above the basin in your
bathroom," says the
receptionist.

Question and Answer Session

Q: How do you get an idiot to
    burn his ear?
A: *Phone him up while he's*
    doing his ironing.

Q: How do you start
   a pudding race?
A: *Sago!*

Q: How do you keep an
    idiot in suspense?
A: *I'll tell you later.*

Q: How does a blind skydiver know when he's approaching the ground?
A: *His dog's lead goes slack.*

Q: How do you make an idiot laugh on Monday?
A: *Tell him a joke on Friday.*

Q: **How do you make a chainsaw sound like a set of bagpipes?**
A: ***Add vibrato.***

Q: How do you sink a submarine full of idiots?
A: *Knock on the door.*

Old Riddles

Q: Two legs I have, and this will
    confound: only at rest do they
    touch the ground! What am I?
A: *A wheelbarrow.*

> Q: What has roots that nobody
>   sees, and is taller than trees?
>   Up, up it goes, and yet it
>   never grows. What is it?
> A: *A mountain.*

Q: Give it food and it will
    live; give it water and
    it will die. What is it?
A: *Fire.*

Q: The more there is of it, the less you will see. What is it?
A: *Darkness.*

Q: What can run but never walks, has a mouth but never talks, has a head but never weeps, has a bed but never sleeps?

A: *A river.*

Telling Twins Apart

A man tells his friend that his wife is one of twins. "It must be difficult telling them apart," says the friend. "Oh, it is," says the man. "Especially now her brother's shaved his beard off."

The Mother-in-law's Funeral

A funeral director asks a man, "Would you like your late mother-in-law buried, created or embalmed?" "I'm taking no chances," says the man. "Give her the lot!"

When Does The Smoke Alarm Go Off

The Fire Brigade are doing a demonstration in the local school. The fire chief asks the children, "Does anyone know what it means when the smoke alarm goes off." "Yes, sir!" says a little boy putting his hand up. "My dad's cooking dinner!"

You Should Be On TV

A man is listening to his niece caterwauling away. At the end of her rendition he says, "You know what? You should be on TV!" "Do you really think I'm that good?" asks the niece. "Not really," says the man. "But at least then I'd be able to switch you off."

Farmer Giles And The Vicar's Sermon

One morning at church there is only one person in the congregation, Farmer Giles. The vicar is disappointed with the turnout and has a word with the farmer to ask if he'd mind if the service was cancelled for today.

"Yes I would mind!" says Farmer Giles. "If I go out in the farmyard with my bucket of corn to feed my hens and only one of them comes running, I don't let that one hen go hungry."

"That's a good point, Farmer Giles!" says the vicar.

Inspired by the farmer's words, the vicar gets up and not only performs the service but gives Giles the very best he can offer.

After a forty-five minute sermon, three readings and five hymns the vicar stands at the church door as the farmer leaves.

"Enjoy the service, Farmer Giles?" asks the vicar.

"No I did not!" says Giles.

"But," says the vicar, "you said when you go out in the farmyard with your bucket of corn and only one hen comes running, you still feed that one hen!"

"I know I did," says the farmer. "But if only one hen turns up, I don't give her the whole flipping bucket!"

Various Professional People's Daughters

She was only a clergyman's daughter but you couldn't put anything pastor.

She was only an electrician's daughter but she had all the right connections.

She was only a milkman's daughter, but she was still the cream of the crop.

She was only a fisherman's daughter, but she reeled when she saw my rod.

She was only a lighthouse
keeper's daughter, but she
never went out at night.

> She was only a film censor's
> daughter, but she didn't
> know when to cut it out.

She was only a teacher's
daughter, but she taught
all the boys a lesson.

> She was only a flag-wavers
> daughter, but she'd let her
> standards down for anyone.

She was only a violinist's daughter,
but when she removed her G-string,
all the boys wanted a fiddle.

The Lost Dog

A man loses a rare and valuable dog. He places an advert in the local newspaper offering a reward of £5,000 for the animal's return. He is confident that this sizeable sum will encourage someone to come forward with information and yet no-one contacts him. In the end he calls the paper to check his advert has appeared. No-one answers his call so he crossly puts on his coat and sets off to the newspaper office. At the office he asks the receptionist if he might see the classified ads manager.

"I'm sorry sir," says the receptionist. "But he's out of the office."

"OK," says the man. "Could I see his secretary?"

"I'm sorry, sir," says the receptionist. "She's out of the office too."

"Right!" says the man. "I want to see the editor."

"I'm sorry, sir," says the receptionist. "But the editor is out as well."

"I can't believe this?" says the man. "Where are all the people who are supposed to be working on this newspaper?"

"Well, if you must know," says the receptionist, "they're all out looking for your dog!"

A Trip Somewhere New

A man tells his friend, "Today's my wife's
birthday and for months she's been asking
me to take her somewhere she's never been
before." "So where did you take her?" asks the
friend. "Our kitchen!" says the man.

Are There Any Policemen Around

A man runs up to another man in the street and says,
"Have you seen a policeman around here anywhere?"
"No," says the man. "You never see the police around
here." "Good!" says the other. "Stick 'em up!"

Do Not Disturb

A man phones the reception of a hotel.
"Help!" he says, "I appear to be trapped
in my room." "That's impossible," says the
receptionist. "No," says the man. "There are
only three doors in here. One is the wardrobe,
one is the bathroom and the other one has a
'Do not disturb' sign hanging on it!"

The Nude Painting

A woman goes to a painter and says, "Could you
paint me in the nude." "OK," says the painter.
"But I might have to keep my socks on otherwise
I'll have nowhere to put my brushes."

Old Riddles

Q: How far can a dog run into the woods?

A: *Only halfway because after that he will be running out of the woods.*

Q: It is the beginning of eternity, the end of time and space, the beginning of the end, and the end of every space?

A: *The letter 'e'.*

Q: You can carry it
everywhere you
go, and it does not
get heavy. What is it?
A: *Your name.*

Q: I am weightless, but
you can see me. Put
me in a bucket, and
I'll make it lighter.
What am I?
A: *A hole.*

Q: I'm light as a feather, yet
the strongest man can't
hold me for much more
than a minute. What am I?
A: *Breath.*

Two Toothbrush Salesmen

Two toothbrush salesmen are talking. One is very successful and sells thousands of toothbrushes each week. The other is desperate to find out his secret.

"Well," says the first salesman, "What I do is set up a stall in the market square; I place this bowl of hummus on the table in front of me and beside it a plate of crackers. Then I ask the passers-by if they would like to try my free crackers and dip."

"That's stupid," says the other salesman. "How is that going to help you sell toothbrushes?"

"Well, why not try some?" says the first and the other salesman takes a cracker, dips it in the hummus and tastes it.

"Aagh!" he cries out. "This hummus tastes like cow manure!"

"Well, there's a simple explanation for that," says the first salesman. "It *is* cow manure. Want to buy a toothbrush?"

Question and Answer Session

Q: What's a Hindu?
A: *Lay eggs.*

Q: What's white, furry
   and smells of mint?
A: *A polo bear.*

Q: What is pink and hard?
A: *A pig with a flick knife.*

Q: Why shouldn't you play
cards in the jungle?
A: *Too many cheetahs.*

Q: What sort of dog can
jump higher than a
building?
A: *Any kind of dog. Buildings
can't jump.*

Q: What do you call a
chicken in a shell
suit?
A: *An egg.*

Q: What do you call a
monkey in a minefield?
A: *A baboom.*

Strange Man In The Kitchen

A little boy runs to his mother shouting, "Mummy! Mummy! Come quick! There's a strange man in the kitchen kissing the au pair girl." His mum leaps up looking alarmed at which point the little boy says, "Ha ha! Fooled you! There is no strange man. It's daddy!"

The Love Bird Collar

An old lady buys a pair of lovebirds but when she gets them home she can't remember which is the male and which the female. She asks for advice and a friend tells her, "What you need to do is wait until they're getting frisky then grab the one that's on top and pop a little band round its neck. Then you will know which one is the male!" The old lady does this and successfully collars the male bird. A few days later the vicar calls round for tea. The vicar goes over to the cage to look at the birds and the male looks at his collar and says, "So, they caught you as well did they, mate?"

The Relative Weight Of Married and Single Ladies

Why are married women heavier than single women? Single women come home, look what's in the fridge and go to bed. Married women come home, look what's in bed and go to the fridge.

Police Investigations

After a number of people have been found stabbed with knitting needles, police believe the crimes may be following some kind of pattern.

A consignment of wigs has been stolen. Police are combing the area.

A lorry load of prunes have been stolen. Police say the thieves are still on the run.

The police have found a wanted man holding out in a public convenience. Eventually they managed to flush him out.

Police say a criminal midget clairvoyant has escaped from prison. They're looking for a small medium at large.

Old Riddles

Q: Twelve white ponies,
   On a red hill, Always
   moving, but standing still.
   What are they?

A: *Teeth.*

Q: Can you translate
   the following?
   Y Y U R Y Y U B I
   C U R Y Y 4 M E.

A: *Two wise you are,*
   two wise you be,
   I see you are two wise
   for me.

Q: In a marble hall white as milk, Lined with skin as soft as silk. Within a fountain crystal-clear, A golden apple doth appear. No doors there are to this stronghold, Yet thieves break in to steal its gold. What is it?

A: *An egg.*

Q: What gets wetter and wetter the more it dries?

A: *A towel.*

Q: I have holes in my top and bottom, my left and right, and in the middle. But I still hold water. What am I?

A: *A sponge.*

Three Men And A Genie

Three guys have been stuck on a deserted island for years. One day one of them finds a lamp on the beach. He picks it up and gives it a rub and a genie appears.

The genie looks at the three men and tells them, "Normally it's three wishes for one person, but since there are three of you, I will grant each of you a separate wish."

The first man says, "I am thoroughly sick and tired of being on the island so I wish I was back home with my wife and family."

And with a flash he is gone.

The next man says, "I'm also sick and tired of being on this island so I also wish I was back home."

And with a flash he is gone.

The third man says, "Aw! It's a bit lonely here on the island all by myself. I wish my two mates were back here with me..."

A Yorkshire Man At The Vet's

A Yorkshire man goes to the vet and says, "Eee, I've come to see thee because I'm right worried about me cat." "Oh aye," says the vet. "So is it a tom?" "No," says the Yorkshire Man. "It's 'ere in this basket."

Question and Answer Session

Q: How do you know if you're ugly?

A: *Your dog keeps its eyes closed while it's humping your leg.*

Q: How do you catch a bra?

A: *Set a booby trap.*

Q: How do you disperse a mob of angry Scotsmen?

A: *Charge at them holding a collection box.*

Q: How do you make an old lady say a rude word?
A: *Say "Bingo"!*

Q: **How do you confuse an idiot?**
A: ***Tell him to count the stairs on an escalator.***

Q: How do you make a hormone?
A: *Don't pay her.*

Q: How do you make holy water?
A: *Boil the hell out of it.*

Three Times Unfaithful

A couple are celebrating their golden wedding anniversary. The husband takes the opportunity to ask his wife whether in all their years together she has ever been unfaithful to him.

"Only three times," she says.

"Three times!" says the husband horrified.

"Yes," says the wife, "but listen – remember that time you couldn't get a loan to get the business started? I went to the bank manager and I slept with him and the next day he offered you the money."

"My darling!" says the man. "You made that sacrifice for me? How wonderful. What about the second time?"

"Well," says the wife, "remember when you needed that operation but we couldn't afford to pay for it? I went to the surgeon, I slept with him and the next day he did that operation for you free of charge."

"I don't know what to say," says the man. "You are the most wonderful wife a man could have. What about the third time?"

"Well," says the wife. "Remember that time you wanted to be president of the golf club but you needed 87 of the members to vote for you?"

Elephants

Q: Why don't elephants
like penguins?
A: *They can't get the
silver paper off.*

Q: Why do elephants wear
yellow shoes?
A: *So they can hide upside
down in a bowl of custard.*

Q: Have you ever seen an
elephant upside down in
a bowl of custard?
A: *No, because they're
wearing yellow shoes.*

Q: Why do elephants live in herds?
A: *So they can get a bulk discount on orders of yellow shoes.*

Q: What's grey, yellow, grey, yellow, grey, yellow, grey, yellow, grey, yellow, grey, yellow?
A: *An elephant rolling down a hill with a daisy in its mouth!*

Q: What's grey and white on the inside and red on the outside?
A: *An inside out elephant.*

Q: Why have elephants got big ears?
A: *Because Noddy won't pay the ransom.*

The Woman Stowaway

A young woman in Southampton is so depressed that she decides to end it all by throwing herself from a bridge.

As she is about to leap, a handsome sailor spots her and takes pity on her.

He tells her, "You have a lot to live for. I'm off to America in the morning, and if you like, I'll stow you away on the ship. I'll take good care of you and bring you food every day."

He moves closer, slips his arm around her and says, "I'll keep you happy if you keep me happy."

The girl cheers up and happily accepts his offer. That night, the sailor brings her aboard the ship and hides her in a lifeboat. Then every night he brings her a sandwich and a drink and they make mad passionate love until dawn.

Three weeks later, during a routine inspection, the woman is discovered by the captain.

"What are you doing?" asks the captain.

"I have an arrangement with one of your men," explains the woman. "He has stowed me aboard. I get food and free passage to America, and he's screwing me."

"He certainly is," says the captain. "This is the Isle of Wight Ferry!"

A Man Parking His Car

A man parks his car. Just as he is getting out, a traffic warden walks up and says, "I'm sorry, sir. You can't park your car here." "Yes I can," says the man. "The sign there says, 'Fine for Parking'!"

The Nude Jogger

Two old men are sitting on a bench outside their retirement home. Suddenly a female resident dashes past them jogging completely in the nude. "What was that?" asks one of the old men. "I think it was old Mavis from room 22," says his friend. "Was it really?" says the first. "What was she wearing?" "I don't know," says the second, "but whatever it was, it definitely needed ironing."

The Christian Thrown To The Lion

At the Colosseum in ancient Rome, a Christian is thrown into the ring to be devoured by a lion. The Christian tries to run around the ring away from the beast but he quickly realizes the lion will soon catch him. Clutching at straws, the Christian turns to face the animal. As it rears up to strike at him, the Christian cries out, "Oh God, I beseech you, turn this lion into a Christian!" Instantly, the lion falls to its knees. "Thank you, oh God, for this miracle!" says the Christian but then notices that the lion is now muttering a quiet prayer: "Oh Lord, for what I am about to receive…"

Question and Answer Session

Q: How do you make a one-armed idiot fall out of a tree?
A: *Wave at him.*

Q: How do you make a Mexican chilli?
A: *Take him to the North Pole.*

Q: How do you spot an idiot in a car wash?
A: *He's the one on a motorbike.*

Q: How do you make an
apple turnover?
A: *Roll it down a hill.*

Q: **How do you make an apple puff?**
A: *Chase it round the garden.*

Q: How do you make
an apple crumble?
A: *Hit it with a
sledgehammer.*

Q: **How do you make a
Venetian blind?**
A: *Poke him in the eye.*

The Private On Sentry Duty

A new soldier is on sentry duty at the regiment's main gate. A large car pulls up with the general sitting in the back. "Halt! Who goes there?" says the sentry. "General Thompson," replies the chauffeur. "Can I see your ID?" asks the new soldier. "Drive on!" calls a cross voice from the back of the car. "But my orders say I have to see everyone's ID or I have to shoot them," says the soldier. "Drive on!" says the general.

The new soldier pokes his head through the back window and says, "Sorry, sir. I'm new at this. Am I supposed to shoot you or the driver?"

Where Do Bad Boys And Girls Go?

One day during the RE lesson, the teacher asks the class, "Does anyone here know where bad little boys and girls go?" A child puts his hand up and says, "Please, miss, is it behind the bike sheds?"

Anniversary Present

A couple are celebrating their wedding anniversary. The husband says, "So what would you like me to get you? A new car? A coat? A diamond necklace?" The wife says, "what I really want is a divorce." "Oh," the husband says, "to be honest, I wasn't planning on spending that much."

All Your Teeth Removed

A man bumps into a friend as he comes out of the dentist's. "Oh," says the man, "I've just had all my teeth taken out. Never again!"

The Man Down A Hole

A man falls down a deep hole. His friend stands at the top looking down. The friend calls down, "Is it very dark down there?" "How am I supposed to know?" says the man. "I can't see a thing."

Two Men Doing
A Crossword Puzzle

Two men are sitting doing a crossword puzzle. The first man reads out a clue: "Overworked postman." "How many letters?" asks the second. "I don't know," says the first. "Presumably thousands."

The Not So Priceless Antiques

A man inherits an ancient violin and an oil painting. He takes them to a valuer who looks at them and says, "Well, this is remarkable. You've got a Stradivarius and a Rembrandt." "Fantastic!" says the man. "So how much are they worth?" "Absolutely nothing," says the valuer. "Stradivarius was a terrible painter and Rembrandt made rotten violins!"

I Think I've Got a Strawberry On My Head

A man goes into the doctor's and says, "Doctor, doctor, I keep thinking I've got a strawberry growing out of the top of my head." "Ah!" says the doctor, "I believe I have some cream you can put on that."

The Same Order
As Last Time

A man walks into a restaurant. The waiter comes over and the man says, "I'd like a cold uncooked sausage served on a greasy plate with a burnt egg and some baked beans that someone has recently sneezed over." "I'm sorry, sir," says the waiter, "we couldn't possibly serve you a meal like that." " Why not?" says the man. "It's what you gave me last time!"

How Much For A Kiss?

A man is chatting up a woman. He asks her, "Would you let me kiss you for a pound?" She says, "Certainly not." He says, "What about for a thousand pounds?" She says, "For a thousand pounds. Yes, I suppose so." He says, "OK. What about for £2.50." "What? No!" says the woman. "What sort of woman do you think I am?" "We've just established what sort of woman you are," says the man. "Now we're just haggling over the price."

The Two Statues

A nude male statue and a nude female statue have been standing facing each other in the middle of the town park for 100 years. An angel sees them and decides to give them a reward. The angel tells the statues, "For enduring 100 blazing summers and 100 freezing winters I am going to make you come to life for one night only so you can do whatever you want."

And with a flash the statues come to life and immediately run off together into the bushes. Sounds of rustling and shrieks of pleasure follow and a few minutes later, the pair emerge into the open.

"You still have some time left," says the angel. "Do you want to do it again?"

"OK," says the female statue to the male statue, "but this time you hold the pigeon down while I crap on it."

The Cat With A Funny Name

A vicar is visiting his parishioners. He knocks on a door and a little girl answers holding a cat. "That's a nice cat," says the vicar. "What's his name?" "He's called Stork Margarine," says the little girl. "That's a funny name for a cat," says the vicar. "Why did you decide to call him that?" "Because," says the little girl, "when I asked my mummy what cooking fat was, she said it was Stork Margarine and when I brought the cat home my daddy said, 'Who brought that cooking fat in here?'"

Question and Answer Session

Q: How do you know if it's
   raining cats and dogs?
A: *You find you've just
   trodden in a poodle.*

Q: **What's green and goes
   up and down?**
A: ***A gooseberry in a lift.***

Q: What do you call a bee
   that's always moaning?
A: *A grumble bee.*

Q: What goes 99 thump, 99 thump?
A: *A centipede with a wooden leg.*

Q: What did one snowman
    say to the other snowman?
A: *"Can you smell carrot?"*

Q: What did one hat say
    to another hat?
A: *"You wait here and I'll
    go on a head."*

Q: What sits at the bottom of
    the ocean and twitches?
A: *A nervous wreck.*

Sherlock Holmes and Dr Watson Go Camping

Sherlock Holmes and Doctor Watson are on a camping holiday. They settle down to sleep on the first night but after a while Watson is woken by his companion nudging him in the ribs.

"Watson," says Holmes, "look up at the stars in the night sky above us and tell me what you deduce."

"Well," says Watson, "I can see thousands upon thousands of stars. Astronomically, this tells me that there are potentially billions of planets. Astrologically, I observe that Saturn is in Leo. And meteorologically, I suspect that we will have a fine day tomorrow with a chance of showers later. What about you, Holmes? What do you deduce from it?"

"That someone has stolen our tent!" says Holmes.

On The Moscow Subway

A man is in a carriage travelling on the Moscow subway. He taps another traveller on the shoulder and says, "Excuse me, comrade, do you work for the police?" "No," says the other traveller. "Oh," says the first, "so do you work for the KGB?" "No," says the other traveller. "Well then," says the first, "are you on the committee of the local communist party or does anyone else in your family work for the Soviet government in any way?" "No they don't," says the other traveller impatiently. "I'm just a simple citizen!" "Well in that case," says the first, "would you stop standing on my foot, you great clumsy idiot!"

Hiding In Trees From The Germans

Three prisoners of war escape and are running away through a forest from the German guards. They decide to hide and they each climb up a tree. The Germans run up to the tree where the first man is hiding and shout, "Ve know you are up zere! Come down viz your handz up!" But the first man decides to trick them and goes, "Toowit, toowit, toowit." The Germans think it's just a bird in the tree so they move on to the next and tell the second man to come down. The second man goes, "T'woo t'woo t'woo." Again the Germans think it's a bird and they move on to the third tree and call, "Ve know you are up zere. Come down viz your handz up!" The third man thinks for a moment and then goes: "Mooo mooo mooo!"

Blind Man At The Door

A woman has just climbed into a nice hot bath when she hears her doorbell ring.

"Who's there?" she calls out of the bathroom window.

"Blind man!" a voice calls back.

She climbs out of the bath and pops downstairs without getting dressed because the poor blind man won't be able to see anything.

She opens the door and the man says, "Cor! Nice tits, love! Now where do you want this blind?

Skoda Jokes

Q: How do you get a
   Skoda to go 70 miles
   per hour?
A: *Push it off Beachy
   Head.*

Q: How do you get a Skoda to
   win a race against a Ferrari?
A: *Push the Skoda off Beachy
   Head first.*

Q: What's the difference between a Jehovah's Witness and a Skoda?

A: You can shut the door on a Skoda.

Replacing The Cat

A man accidentally runs over a cat. He checks the animal's collar and finds its home address. He goes to the house and tells the owner, "I'm very sorry. I'm afraid I've just run over your cat but I'd like to replace him for you." "OK," says the owner. "How are you at catching mice?"

The Old Man In The Ice Cream Parlour

An old man with a bent back hobbles into an ice cream parlour and orders a sundae. The assistant puts a load of toppings on the ice cream. "Crushed nuts, granddad?" he asks. "No," says the bent old man. "It's just rheumatism if you must know."

Phone Call To The Hospital

A man phones up the hospital. "Help!" he says. "My wife has just gone into labour!" "OK," says the nurse, "try and calm down. Now is this her first child?" "No! Don't be stupid!" says the man. "This is her husband!"

Disappointed To Find A Friend In Bed With Your Wife

A man comes home early from work one day and discovers his wife is upstairs in bed with his best friend, Marvin. The man takes the scene in with a look of utter devastation on his face. "Oh, Marvin," he says, "I have to – but you!"

The Passing Funeral Procession

Two men are fishing by the riverbank. A funeral procession passes by over the bridge. One of the men stands up, takes off his cap and solemnly holds it to his chest. When he sits down again, his friend says, "That was a nice gesture." "Well," says the first fisherman, "it was the least I could do. She was a good wife to me."

The Young Subaltern

A young subaltern joins a new regiment. The commanding officer greets him and says, "Welcome to the regiment. On Wednesday nights we always have a little party in the mess where you can get to know everyone over a few drinks."

"I'm sorry, sir," says the subaltern, "but I'm afraid I don't drink."

"Oh. Never mind," says the CO, "well how about Friday night instead then? On Fridays we always get a few girls up to the mess from the NAAFI for a dance and bit of slap and tickle."

"Once again I'm sorry, sir," says the subaltern, "but that's not my kind of thing either."

The CO gives the subaltern a quizzical look. "Are you one of those fellows who enjoys intimate relations with other men?"

"Why no, sir!" says the subaltern extremely embarrassed. "I most certainly am not!"

"Oh dear," says the CO. "So you're not going to enjoy Saturday night either."

Elephants

Q: How do you smuggle an
   elephant across the border?
A: *Put a slice of bread on each
   side, and call him "lunch".*

Q: How can you tell if an
   elephant is under your
   bed?
A: *The ceiling is very close!*

Q: What time is it when an
   elephant sits on your fence?
A: *Time to build a new fence.*

Q: Why are elephants covered in wrinkles?
A: *Have you ever tried to iron one?*

Q: Why won't they allow elephants in public swimming pools?
A: *Because they might let down their trunks.*

Q: What do you give a seasick elephant?
A: *Plenty of room.*

Q: What's the difference between an elephant and a digestive biscuit?
A: *Have you ever tried dipping an elephant in your cup of tea?*

Q: How do you know if there is an elephant in the pub?
A: *Its bike is locked up outside.*

The Vacuum Cleaner Injury

A man has to be rushed to hospital after injuring himself while messing around with the vacuum cleaner. His wife phones the hospital the next day to ask how he is. "Oh," says the nurse, "he's picking up."

Three Socks

A lady bumps into a friend in the Post Office and asks her, "Why are you sending your son three socks rather than a pair?" "Well," says the friend, "he wrote to me that since he's been in the army, he's grown another foot."

The Talking Parrot

After years of painstaking work a man teaches his parrot not only to speak, but to recite the entire soliloquy from *Hamlet*. After all this effort, the man decides to capitalise on the matter and takes his parrot to the pub, where he bets everyone the bird can recite *Hamlet*'s "To be or not to be" speech. There is a lot of interest and a stack of money is piled on the bar. "Right, go on then, Polly!" says the man. "Do 'To be or not to be'!" But to his frustration the parrot remains completely silent. Back at home having lost a small fortune, the man is furious. "You feathery git!" he yells. "After all these years of training! Why couldn't you have done what I taught you?" "Calm down," says the parrot, "Just think of the odds we'll get when we go back tomorrow night!"

I Think I'm A Pony

A man goes into the doctor's and says, "Doctor, I think I'm a pony." "Nonsense, man!" says the doctor. "You're just a little hoarse."

Saving For Retirement

A man comes home and tells his wife that he has lost his job because he is too old. "Now," he says, "I'm not sure how we're going to survive on my pension." "Well, says the wife, "we have a little money put aside." "How did we manage that?" asks the husband. "Well, ever since we were married, every time we made love I got you to give me £10. You thought it was just for housekeeping and clothes but I put it all in the bank ready for when you're no longer working. We've now got nearly £30,000 saved up." "Damn!" says the husband. "If only I'd known you were doing that, I'd have given you all my business!"

If You Were Stranded
On A Desert Island

A man asks his friend, "Out of all the people in the world, who would you most like to be stuck on a desert island with?" "Oh. That's easy," says the friend. "I'd choose my Uncle Bert." "Why's that?" asks the man. "Because he's got a boat," says the friend.

The Science of Worms

A man is lecturing on the virtues of temperance and the damage that alcohol can do. To demonstrate, he holds up a worm and puts it in a glass of water. After floating in the glass of water for a few moments the worm is still alive. The man takes the worm out and drops it into a glass of whisky. After a few moments in the whisky, the worm is dead. "So," says the man, "we can all learn a lesson from this." "Yes," calls a voice from the back of the hall, "if you drink whisky, you won't get worms!"

The Sailing Lecture

A young man is a member of a local club. One night the club decides to have an evening where each of the members will speak on a subject drawn at random from a hat. The young man pulls a piece of paper from the hat and discovers he has to do his speech on the subject of sex. When he gets home that evening he is too embarrassed to tell his wife what happened at the club and so instead tells her that he had to make a speech on the subject of sailing.

A few days later another member of the club bumps into the man's wife and tells her, "That was a marvellous talk your husband gave us the other night."

"That's funny," says the wife. "I wouldn't have thought he knew much about the subject at all. He's only done it twice. The first time he was sick and the second time his hat blew off!"

Did You Hear About...

Did you hear about the flasher who was thinking of retiring?
In the end he decided to stick it out for another year.

Did you hear about the "morning after" pill they've just invented for men?
It changes their blood type.

Did you hear about the pregnant librarian?
Her baby was two weeks overdue so she got a 75p fine.

Did you hear about the Rear Admiral who fell into a vat of fresh whipped cream?
He's just been piped aboard ship.

Did you hear about the man who drowned in a bowl of breakfast cereal?
A strong currant pulled him under.

Did you hear about the man who fell into the upholstery machine?
He's fully recovered now.

The Empty Bottle
Of Milk In The Fridge

A man is at his friend's house
when he notices something inside
his friend's fridge door. "Why have
you got an empty bottle of milk in
your fridge?" asks the man. "Oh,"
says the friend, "that's in case
anyone wants a black coffee."

Stripping Wallpaper

A man visits a miserly friend whom
he finds carefully stripping his
wallpaper off. "Are you doing some
decorating?" asks the man. "No,"
says his friend, "I'm moving."

The Wartime Paratroopers

During the war a group of soldiers are getting ready to parachute behind German lines. Their sergeant major guides them to the aeroplane door one by one and pushes them out. As he does so the sergeant major shouts, "Come on! Come on! No time to mess around! Out you go!" One of the men however attempts to resist being pushed out of the plane. "Come on! You disgusting coward!" says the sergeant major pushing the man towards the door. "No time to mess around! Out you go!" Finally the sergeant major gives the man an almighty kick and launches him out of the plane. The rest of the men are by this stage in stitches laughing. "You think that was funny, do you?" says the sergeant major. "Well," says one of the men, "not that funny. That was the pilot."

The Chainsaw

A man walks into a hardware shop to buy a chainsaw. The salesman shows him the top of the range model. "With this," says the salesman, "you will be able to cut down 20 trees a day." A few days later the man is back. "You told me this chainsaw would cut down 20 trees a day," he tells the salesman. "I took it out the first day and barely managed to cut down two very thin trees. The next day I tried again. I got up at 4 in the morning, worked as hard as I could all day and still only managed to cut through 3 very thin trees." "Oh dear," says the salesman, "it sounds like this chainsaw may be defective in some way. Let's just give it a try and see what's wrong." The salesman then plugs the chainsaw in and starts it up at which point the man asks, "What's that noise?"

The Dress In The Window

A woman walks into a clothes shop and says, "Could I try on that dress in the window?" "You can if you want," says the sales assistant, "but customers usually prefer the changing room."

Three Minutes To Live

A man is in hospital being examined by a doctor. "I'm afraid to tell you," says the doctor, "that you've only got three minutes to live." "Oh dear," says the man. "Is there anything you can do for me?" "Well," says the doctor, "I could boil you an egg."

Two Nuns In Transylvania

Two nuns are on a sightseeing trip driving through Transylvania. A vampire suddenly jumps in front of the car causing them to slam on the brakes. The nun in the driving seat panics. She turns to her companion and says, "Quick, sister! Show him your cross!"

So the nun in the passenger seat winds her window down and yells, "Get off out of the way, you ugly pointy toothed bastard!"

The Unmarried Couple On A Cruise

An unmarried couple go on a cruise. A storm blows up and the ship is smashed apart by enormous waves. The couple are left hanging onto a piece of wood for dear life. After two days in the water with nothing to eat or drink, the man is getting desperate and cries out to God, "Lord, please save us. Show us mercy and spare our lives. If we survive I promise I will give up smoking, drinking, gambling, swearing…" Just at that moment his girlfriend nudges him in the ribs and whispers, "Better leave it there. I think we're approaching land."

The Wrong Number

A man calls a wrong number at three o'clock in the morning. "Hello," he says, "is that the Farmer's Arms?" "No it's not," says a voice, "this is a private residence." "Oh. I must have dialled the wrong number," says the man, "I'm sorry to have troubled you." "Oh it's no trouble," says the voice, "I had to get up to answer the phone anyway."

What Do You Call....

What do you call a
woman with one leg?
Eileen.

What do you call a Mexican
who has lost his car?
Carlos.

What do you call a Chinese
woman with one leg?
Irene.

**What do you call a
French man in sandals?**
Philippe Philoppe.

What do you call a woman with
a screwdriver in one hand, a knife
in the other, scissors between the
toes on one foot and a corkscrew
between the toes on the other?
A Swiss Army wife.

What do you call a
man with his right arm
in a shark's mouth?
Lefty.

Everyone Thinks I'm a Liar

A man goes into the doctor's and says, "Doctor, I keep feeling that everyone thinks I'm a liar." "I find that very hard to believe," says the doctor.

The New Dog

A man phones up his friend and asks him to come over to play with his new dog. "OK," says the friend. "Does the dog bite?" "That's what I want to find out," says the man.

The Motorcyclist's Passenger

A motorcyclist gives a friend a lift on the back of his bike. It is however a particularly cold day so the motorcyclist tells his friend the best way to keep warm is to take off his overcoat and put it on backwards. Once his friend has put his coat on as suggested, the pair set off. Their route takes them along a very bumpy country lane. After a few minutes bumping along the road, the motorcyclist looks behind him and notices that his friend has fallen off the bike. He turns round and goes back to look for him. Eventually he finds his friend lying in the road surrounded by a group of farm labourers who have stopped to help. "Is he alright?" asks the motorcyclist. "Well, he was," says one of the labourers, "until we turned his head round the right way."

Question and Answer Session

Q: What's black and white and
black and white and black
and white and black and
white?

A: *A penguin rolling down a hill.*

Q: What's black and
white and laughing?

A: *The penguin that
pushed him.*

Q: What's black and white
and red all over?

A: *An embarrassed zebra.*

Q: What did the buffalo
say to his male offspring
before leaving for work in
the morning?
A: *Bison.*

Q: **What do you call a
donkey with three legs?**
A: ***A wonkey.***

Q: How many ears does
Davy Crockett have?
A: *Three – a left ear, a right
ear and a wild front ear.*

Q: **What's big, red and
sits in the corner?**
A: ***A naughty bus.***

Called Up For National Service

A young man is called up for National Service. At his medical he tells the examiner he doesn't believe he is fit to serve because of his poor eyesight. The examiner tries various eye tests and the young man fails each of them. In the end the examiner holds up a dustbin lid and says, "Can you tell me what this is?" "It's either a half crown," says the young man, "or it's a two shilling piece." After being officially confirmed as unfit to serve, the young man celebrates by going to the local cinema. A couple of minutes into the film however, the young man is horrified to see the examiner walk into the cinema and sit down beside him. The pair instantly recognize each other but the young man quick as a flash thinks to say, "I am on the right bus for Bromley aren't I?"

Sleeping Together Before Marriage

A man says to a friend, "Call me old fashioned but I didn't sleep with my wife until after we were married. What about you?" "I'm not sure to be honest," says the friend. "What was her maiden name?"

The Two Old Ladies
and The Bunch Of Flowers

Two old ladies are talking. One tells
the other, "My husband brought me a
bunch of flowers last night. You know
what that means? I'm going to have
to spend all weekend with my legs in
the air." "Oh dear," says her friend.
"Haven't you got a vase?"

Two Men Doing A Crossword Puzzle

Two men are sitting doing a crossword puzzle. The first man
reads out a clue: "Found on the bottom of a budgie's cage.
Four letters. Ending in I-T." "Grit!" says the second man.
"Oh yes," says the first. "Can I borrow your rubber?"

A Bear Walks Into a Pub

The bear says, "Could I have
a .... pint
of beer please." "Why the big
pause?" says the barman.
"I don't know," says the bear.
"I was born with them."

People Keep Ignoring Me

A man goes into the doctor's and says, "Doctor, people keep ignoring me." "Next please!" calls the doctor.

Bleeding Ear and Bandaged Feet

A man walks into the doctor's surgery with his ear bleeding and bandages on his feet. "What happened to you?" asks the doctor. "I was opening a can of beans," says the man, "and the instructions said to 'Pierce 'ere and stand in boiling water'."

Drives Like Lightning

A man says to his friend, "My wife drives like lightning." "You mean she's fast," says his friend. "No," says the man. "She keeps hitting trees."

Can I Use Your Toilet

A girl takes a new boyfriend back to her house and tells him to be as quiet as possible so he doesn't wake up her parents who are sleeping upstairs and who have forbidden her from bringing boys home. They snuggle down together on the sofa, but after a moment he says, "Actually I think I need to go the toilet. Where is it?" "Oh dear," she says, "the toilet is next to my parents' bedroom. You can't go there. You'll wake them up. Go in the kitchen and do it in the sink instead." The boyfriend disappears into the kitchen. After a couple of minutes he pops his head round the door and asks, "Have you got any toilet paper?"

Two Men Doing A Crossword Puzzle

Two men are sitting doing a crossword puzzle. The first man reads out another clue. "A female relation. Four letters. Ends in U-N-T." "Aunt," says the second. "Can I borrow that rubber again?" says the first.

A Skeleton Walks Into a Pub

He orders a pint of beer and a mop.

Did You Hear About...

Did you hear about the woman who was having a relationship with a small brigade of soldiers?
She said it was completely platoonic.

Did you hear about the National Dyslexia Association?
It's better known as the DNA.

Did you hear about the Arab dairy farmer?
He's known as the milk sheikh.

Did you hear what they chanted on the dyslexia protest march?
Dyslexics of the world, untie!

Did you hear about the MP who had a dream he was giving a speech in the House of Commons?
He woke up and found he was.

I Think I'm Invisible

A man goes into the doctor's and says, "Doctor, I keep thinking like I'm invisible." "I'm sorry," says the doctor. "I'm afraid I can't see you right now."

I Still Think I'm Invisible

A man goes into the doctor's and says, "Doctor, I still keep thinking I'm invisible." "Who said that?" says the doctor.

The Vial Of Cyanide

A woman walks into a chemist and asks to buy a bottle of cyanide. The pharmacist is somewhat taken aback and asks what she wants the poison for. "I want to kill my husband," says the woman. "I'm terribly sorry, madam," replies the pharmacist, "but under the circumstances I cannot sell you any cyanide." "Really," says the woman, "then have a look at this!" And with that the woman whips out a photograph of her husband in bed with the pharmacist's wife. "Forgive me, madam," says the pharmacist, "I didn't realize you had a prescription!"

The Enormous Contraceptive Pill

A woman with eight children goes to the doctor because she doesn't want to get pregnant by accident again. "OK, I'd better give you one of these contraceptive pills," says the doctor, and rolls in a pill that is six feet in diameter. "How am I supposed to take that?" asks the woman. "You don't take it," says the doctor. "You just roll it against the bedroom door to stop your husband getting in."

Counterfeit

A policeman is in the witness box in court giving evidence. "This woman came up to me when I was in plain clothes," says the policeman, "and she tried to pass off this fake ten pound note." "Counterfeit?" asks the judge. "Yes," says the policeman consulting his notebook. "She had two."

The Auctioned Parrot

A sailor goes to an auction and a parrot comes up for sale. The sailor thinks he'd like the parrot so he calls out a bid of "£50". As soon as he does so another voice calls out "£70." "£80!" bids the sailor. "£90!" the other voice calls out immediately. The sailor becomes determined not to be outbid and the pair carry on bidding against one another until before long the price has been pushed up to £1,000. "That's a lot of money I've had to pay for this bird," says the sailor as he collects the parrot from the auctioneer. "After all that, I hope he can talk." "Of course he can," says the auctioneer. "Who do you think was bidding against you?"

Chauffeur Suicide

A rich old man is out in his car one day. The old man leans forward and says to the chauffeur, "James, I'm extremely old and tired of life now. I've decided I wish to commit suicide. Would you drive me over that cliff please!"

A Friend Of The Bride's

A fierce looking woman walks into the church where a wedding service is due to begin. "Good afternoon, madam," says one of the ushers. "Are you a friend of the bride?" "Definitely not!" says the woman. "I am the groom's mother!"

Chatting Up A Lesbian

A man is in a bar when he notices a young woman sitting on her own. "I think I might go and try chatting her up," he tells the barman. "You'll get nothing there," says the barman. "She's a lesbian." "Just watch me!" says the man as he walks over to the woman, sits down next to her and asks her, "So, darling, which part of Lesbia are you from?"

Back Home From The Dentist

A man gets home after a visit to the dentist. "Does your tooth still hurt?" asks his wife. "I'm not sure," says the man. "The dentist kept it."

Long Sentence

An old man up in court is found guilty and sentenced to 15 years in prison. "But I won't live to do it!" says the man. "Don't worry!" says the judge. "Just do as much as you can!"

Changing Light Bulbs

Q: How many lawyers does it take to change a light bulb?

A: *How many can you afford?*

Q: How many Irishmen does it take to change a light bulb?

A: *Twenty-one – one to hold the bulb and 20 to drink until the room spins.*

Q: How many punk rockers does it take to change a light bulb?

A: *Two. One to change the bulb, and one to eat the old one.*

Q: How many motor mechanics does it take to change a light bulb?

A: *Six. One to force it in with a hammer and five to go out for some more bulbs.*

Q: How many rock stars does it take to change a light bulb?

A: *Twenty. One to hold the bulb, two to turn the ladder, and seventeen on the guest list.*

Q: How many statisticians does it take to change a light bulb?

A: *How many did it take this time last year?*

Q: How many bureaucrats does it take to change a light bulb?

A: *45 – one to change the bulb; 44 to do the paperwork.*

Aphrodisiac Rhino Horn

Two young women are discussing their husbands. One complains that her husband is somewhat lacking in sexual prowess.

"My husband used to be like that as well," says her friend. "But then I started giving him some of this aphrodisiac powdered rhino horn and his performance has become much improved."

The first young woman gets hold of some of the rhino horn and decides her husband needs a substantial dose each day. A month later they meet again and her friend asks her if the rhino horn worked.

"Oh yes," says the first woman, "my husband has become an insatiable lover. The only trouble is when we're out walking, every time he sees a Land Rover he tries to charge it!"

The Infirm Old German

An elderly German man suddenly falls over in the street. Some people gather round to help.

"Are you alright, sir?" says one man.

"Oh yez," says the old German. "I zeemed to just zuffer a dizzy zpell and zo I vell over."

"Oh dear," says the man. "Have you got vertigo?"

"Not really," says the old German man. "I only live just round zer corner!"

I've Swallowed a Roll of Film

A man goes into the doctor's and says, "Doctor, I've swallowed a roll of film." "OK," says the doctor. "Take these pills, then come back tomorrow and we'll see what develops."

The Man With Holes In His Willy

A man goes into a public toilet but when he starts weeing it sprays out in all directions. "Ugh!" says the man at the next urinal. "You've got to get something done about that! It's going everywhere! Look at it! It's got holes up and down the sides!"

And so the man goes to the doctor and shows him his problem. "Oh dear," says the doctor as he writes down a name and address on a card. "This is the name of someone I think you should go and see."

"Thank you, doctor," says the man taking the card. "So is this person some kind of specialist?"

"No," says the doctor, "he's a clarinet player. He'll teach you how to hold it."

The Return Ticket

A man goes up to a train ticket office. "I'd like a return ticket please," says the man. "Certainly, sir," says the employee of the railway company. "Where to?" "Back here of course," says the man.

The Unexpected Music Hall Act

Two sailors on shore leave go to a music hall variety show. They have a few drinks before the performance begins and by the interval one of them desperately needs to go to the toilet. He asks for directions from the usher who tells him to walk down the aisle, through the doors, turn right, turn left, turn right again and down the corridor. Being slightly lightheaded from the drink the sailor gets lost on the way but nevertheless finds a brightly lit toilet where he relieves himself. Eventually he finds his way back to his seat and asks his friend if he has missed any good acts. "Yes," says his friend, "you missed the best one of all. While you were away a sailor came on stage, unzipped his pants in front of the entire audience and proceeded to pee into the orchestra pit for five minutes!"

My Hands Keep Shaking

A man goes into the doctor's and says, "Doctor, my hands keep shaking." "Do you drink much?" asks the doctor. "Not really," says the man. "I tend to spill most of it."

Boosting The Wife's Confidence

A wife is standing naked looking into her bedroom mirror. She says to her husband, "Look at me. I'm ugly, I'm fat. Make me feel better about myself! Pay me a compliment." "Well," says her husband, "your eyesight seems pretty good!"

Question and Answer Session

Q: What's big, hairy and
   sticks out of your pyjamas?
A: *Your head.*

Q: What's red and bad
   for your teeth?
A: *A brick.*

Q: What's big, green
   and can't fly?
A: *A field.*

Q: What's plastic, filled with
   sandwiches and found in a French
   cathedral?
A: *The lunch pack of Notre Dame.*

Q: What do you give the
   man who has everything?
A: *Penicillin.*

Q: What's 30 foot long
   and lives on potatoes?
A: *The queue at a Moscow
   butcher's.*

Q: What is green, has four
   legs and if it fell out of a
   tree it would kill you?
A: *A snooker table.*

Q: What goes blonde brunette
   blonde brunette blonde
   brunette?
A: *A blonde doing cartwheels.*

School Reunion

Bob and Bill meet for the first time in years at a school reunion. Bob asks Bill, "How has life treated you?" "Not so bad," says Bob, "I set up a business and now we have branches all over the country. I have a beautiful house and a lovely wife." "Very good," says Bill, "and what line of business are you in?" "I'm an estate agent," says Bob. "But what about you? How has life treated you?" "Not so well really," says Bill. "After leaving school I set up a business and then married my childhood sweetheart but a week later she left me for my best man. Then my house burnt down, my parents died in a plane crash and this morning my doctor just told me I've got a terrible terminal disease and I've only got 2 weeks to live." "Oh dear," says Bob, "so what line of business was it you went into?" "I sell lucky charms," says Bill.

I Think I'm a Sheep

A man goes into the doctor's
and says, "Doctor, I think
I'm a sheep." "How do
you feel?" asks the doctor.
"Quite baaa-aad,"
says the man.

A Card Game With Africans

A man bumps into a friend. "I've
just been playing cards with some
fellows from Africa," he says.
"Zulus?" says the friend. "No," says
the man, "most of the time
I won."

Knock Knock

Knock Knock!
Who's there?
Booo!
Booo who?
Don't cry, its only a joke!

Knock Knock!
Who's there?
A little old lady.
A little old lady who?
I didn't know you could
yodel!

Knock Knock!
Who's there?
Atch.
Atch who?
Bless you!

Knock, Knock!
Who's there?
Police.
Police who?
Police stop telling these
terrible knock, knock jokes!

Farmer Giles And The Man From The Ministry

A government inspector arrives on Farmer Giles' farm.

He says, "I've come to do a spot check to make sure you're running the farm according to official guidelines. You must therefore allow me access to all parts of the farm."

"Very well," says Farmer Giles. "Except you can't go into the bottom field."

"I'm sorry you're taking this attitude," says the inspector, producing a piece of paper from his briefcase. "But this document gives me permission to go anywhere I like on your farm with or without your say so."

"Very well," says Farmer Giles. "But I still don't want you to go in the bottom field."

"Right!" says the inspector. "The bottom field is the very first place I'm going to go and this document prohibits you from stopping me."

The inspector storms off towards the bottom field and the farmer sits down with a cup of tea.

Ten minutes later, Farmer Giles wanders down to the bottom field where the inspector is being chased round and round through the mud by Giles' prize bull.

"What should I do?!" cries the inspector.

"Quick!" shouts Farmer Giles. "Show him your bit of paper!"

Lottery Winner

A man calls his wife and says, "I've won the lottery! Quick! Get packing?" "OK," says his wife. "So am I packing for hot weather or cold?" "I don't care," says the husband, "just as long as you're gone by the time I get home!"

I Snore Loudly

A man goes into the doctor's and says, "Doctor, you've got to help me. I snore so loudly I keep myself awake." "I see," says the doctor. "So have you tried sleeping in a different room?"

The Noisy Chess Enthusiasts

A group of semi-professional chess players check into a hotel. They then stand for an hour or more talking loudly about all their recent victories on the semi-professional chess playing circuit.

Eventually the hotel manager cannot stand this any longer. He stomps out of his office and orders the group to disperse.

"But why," asks one of the group. "What have we done?"

"I'll tell you why," says the manager, "it's because I simply cannot bear chess-nuts boasting in an open foyer."

Piano Tuner At The Door

A man answers his front door and finds a piano tuner waiting on the step. "I didn't order a piano tuner," says the man. "I know you didn't," says the piano tuner. "But your neighbours did."

The Scouser Learning Urdu

A scouser walks into a library and asks for a book called "An Introduction To Urdu". The librarian asks, "Are you going to India on holiday?" "No," says the scouser. "I want to learn how to be a hairdresser."

The Man With The Steering Wheel Sticking Out Of His Trousers

A man walks into the doctor's with a small steering wheel sticking out of the front of his trousers. "What's that?" asks the doctor. "I don't know," says the man. "But it's driving me nuts."

Buying A Labrador

A man says to his friend, "I'm thinking of getting myself a Labrador." "No! Don't get one of those," says the friend. "Have you seen how many of the owners end up going blind?"

William Shakespeare Walks Into a Pub

"Hey, Shakespeare!" says the barman. "I've told you before. You're bard!"

In A Vacuum

A man asks his friend, "If you're in a vacuum and someone calls your name, can you hear them?" "It depends," says the friend. "Is the vacuum switched on or off?"

A White Horse Walks Into a Pub

"Hey," says the barman, "we've got a drink named after you." "What?" says the white horse. "You've got a drink called Steve?"

The Thirteenth Floor

Two burglars are robbing an apartment in a high rise block of flats when they hear the police running up the stairs to catch them. "Quick!" says the first burglar. "We're going to have to jump out of the window." "But," says the second, "we're on the thirteenth floor." "Oh for goodness sake!" says the first. "This is no time to be superstitious!"

The Homework About The Pet Dog

A teacher tells a little boy off about his homework. "This essay you wrote about your pet dog," says the teacher, "is exactly the same word for word as the one your brother wrote." "Of course it is," says the boy. "It's the same dog!"

Two Men Doing A Crossword Puzzle

Two men are sitting doing a crossword puzzle. The first man reads a clue: "Completely plain to see. Seven letters. O – blank – V – blank – O – blank – S." "Ah! It's no good," says his friend. "We'll just have to buy tomorrow's newspaper to get the solution."

Buying A Fly Spray

A woman walks into a shop, picks up a can of fly spray and asks, "Is this any good for flies?" "Not really, madam," says the assistant. "It kills them."

The Twelve Inch Pianist

A man walks into a pub and sees a tiny man no more than one foot high playing the piano.

"That's amazing," says the man to the bartender. "Where did you get him?"

"Well," says the bartender, "I've got a genie in a magic lamp here behind the bar and he granted me one wish."

"Wow!" says the man. "So will he grant me a wish as well?"

The bartender produces the magic lamp and the man summons the genie. "Genie," he says, "I want a million pounds!" A moment later the pub is filled with baying dogs.

"No!" the man yells at the genie. "I said a million pounds! Not a million hounds!"

"Yeah, I think he might be a bit deaf," says the bartender. "To be honest, I didn't really ask him for a 12 inch pianist."

A Gorilla Walks Into a Pub

The gorilla orders a pint of beer. "That'll be £4.50," says the barman and then adds, "We don't get many gorillas in this pub." "I'm not surprised at these prices," says the gorilla.

Flaky Pastry

A man is in a restaurant. He calls over the waiter and says, "What happened to the wonderful flaky pastry you served last time I was in here?" "Sorry, sir," says the waiter. "The chef's dermatitis cleared up."

Where's All The Money Going?

A husband says to his wife, "I want to see exactly where all our money is going." "OK," says his wife. "Look in the mirror and turn sideways!"

The Performing Crocodile

A man walks into a pub with a crocodile on a lead. The patrons are horrified and the barman steps forward to protest but the man tells them all, "Don't panic! This crocodile is perfectly trained. Watch this!" And he produces a plank of wood and whacks it down on the crocodile's head. Everyone steps back in horror but the crocodile doesn't react at all. "See!" says the man. "I can do anything I want with him and he's no danger!" And with that the man demonstrates by getting his willy out, putting it into the crocodile's mouth, standing for several moments without sustaining injury and repeatedly hitting the croc over the head with the plank as he does so. "Come on then!" says the man removing his unscratched todger from the croc's mouth. "Who else wants to give it a try?" A little old lady puts her hand up and steps forward, saying, "OK. But just promise me one thing. Don't hit me so hard with the plank!'"

I've Swallowed a Five Pound Note

A man goes into the doctor's and says, "Doctor, help me. I've swallowed a five pound note." "Take these pills," says the doctor, "and give me a call tomorrow if there's been no change."

The Sobbing Man In The Graveyard

A man is passing by a graveyard. He notices another man on his knees by a gravestone crying and apparently distraught. "Oh God!" sobs the man by the gravestone over and over. "Why did you have to go? Why did you have to go?" The passer by goes over to console the man. "Are you alright?" the passer by asks. "Is this your wife's grave?" "No," says the man. "Her first husband's!"

Polish Man At The Optician's

A Polish man goes to have his eyes tested. The optician puts up a chart on the wall in front of him which reads: "Z S N Y X C S F R." "There!" says the optician. "Can you read that?" "Can I read it?" says the Polish man. "I went to school with the guy!"

Prince Charles' Makes An Official Trip To Middlesbrough Wearing A Strange Hat

Prince Charles is on an official visit to Middlesbrough. The mayor welcomes him at the station but notices the prince is wearing a strange red fur hat with a tail hanging down at the side. "Why are you wearing that hat?" asks the mayor. "Well," says the prince, "I told mummy I was going to Middlesbrough and she said, 'Wear the fox hat!'"

Fifty-Nine Seconds to Live

A man goes into the doctor's and says, "Doctor, I've only got 59 seconds to live." "Hold on!" says the doctor. "I shall be with you in a minute."

The Cannibal Canoes

Three men are caught by cannibals. The cannibals tell the men that they are going to skin them, eat them and then use their skins to build canoes. Each of the men is however given a final request.

The first man says, "For my final request I want a pen and some paper." The cannibals grant his request and he writes a farewell letter to his wife.

The second man says, "For my final request I want a bottle of whisky."

Somehow the cannibals find a bottle of whisky and the second man drinks himself unconscious.

Finally the third man steps up and says, "For my final request I want a fork!"

The cannibals look confused but nevertheless they grant his request and hand him a fork. The man grabs the fork off them and immediately starts stabbing himself with it all over his body.

"Ha!" cries the man. "Nobody's using my skin to make a flipping canoe!"

The Prison Joke List

A man is spending his first night in prison. A few minutes after lights out, he hears an inmate from another cell call out, "Thirty-two!" This causes his cellmate and all the prisoners in the other cells to burst out laughing.

After the laughter subsides he hears another inmate call, "Seventy-six!" Once again this produces gales of laughter from the other prisoners.

In the end the man asks his cellmate what's going on.

"Well, you see," says his cellmate, "we've all been in prison so long we know all the jokes off by heart. Now we've given each of them a different number. All we have to do is call out the number of a joke and it sets us off laughing."

"Right," thinks the man, "I can join in with this." So the next time the laughter dies down he calls out, "Forty-three!"

This produces a deafening silence. He tries again but still there is no response. A moment later he hears a voice from one of the other cells call, "Forty-three." This time all the other prisoners roll around laughing.

"I don't understand," says to the man to his cellmate. "Why did no-one laugh when I called out the number, but they fell about laughing when the other man said it?"

"Ah well," says the cellmate. "It's the way he tells them!"